AMAZING INVENTORY OF INCREDIBLE KNOWLEDGE

PUB
TIME

SPORTS

TRIVIA

Publications International, Ltd.

Written By: Marty Strassen

Cover Photo: Shutterstock.com

Louis Weber, CEO
Publications International, Ltd.
7373 North Cicero Avenue
Lincolnwood, Illinois 60712

ISBN-13: 978- 1-4508-7827-2
ISBN-10: 1-4508-7827-X

Manufactured in Canada

8 7 6 5 4 3 2 1

CONTENTS

TRIVIA TIME

Welcome to *Pub Time Sports Trivia*. This is not your typical trivia book. More than just stats, dates, and names, this collection delves into the kind of lore that will stump even the most fanatical sports fan. Think you know all there is to know about obscure rules, clutch performances, and team nicknames? Here's the place to find out.

Pub Time Sports Trivia is organized by sport, making it easy for you to dive right into your favorite pastime. If the gridiron is your thing, you may want to kick off with football. Or perhaps you're a gold medalist in Olympics esoterica. There's something for everyone, whether it's pucks, the pigskin, or points in the paint. You'll find questions on the right-hand pages and answers on the back of each page, along with a few extra tidbits that may teach you a thing or two.

Are you ready? Grab a barstool, pull out *Pub Time Sports Trivia*, and challenge your friends to a few friendly rounds. May the best sports fan win!

HOT LAPS

1. TRUE OR FALSE?

Mario Andretti was the first American to win the Formula One World Championship.

2. WHICH FORMULA ONE WHIZ, NICKNAMED THE "FLYING SCOT," WON AN ASTONISHING 27 OF 99 GRAND PRIX STARTS BEFORE BECOMING A RESPECTED AUTO RACING COMMENTATOR AND SPOKESMAN?

A. Jackie Stewart

B. Nigel Mansell

C. James Hunt

D. Alan Jones

3. NAME THE FIRST FATHER-SON DUO TO FIND VICTORY LANE AT THE INDIANAPOLIS 500.

1.

False. Andretti, in 1978, became the second American to do so. Phil Hill was the first, in 1961.

2.

A. Jackie Stewart was the world's Formula One champ in 1969, '71 and '73.

3.

Al Unser—Sr. and Jr. Al Sr. topped his brother Bobby's two Indy 500 wins with four of his own. Son Al Jr. then became the race's initial second-generation winner when he won his first of two in 1992.

4. MICHAEL SCHUMACHER, AFTER TAKING HIS FORMULA ONE LEGEND RACING FERRARIS TO VICTORY LANE, RETURNED TO THE SPORT IN 2010 WITH WHICH RIVAL TEAM?

A. Red Bull Racing

B. Mercedes

C. McLaren

D. Renault

5. NAME THE BRAZILIAN FORMULA ONE LEGEND WHOSE 1994 DEATH IN A CRASH AT THE SAN MARINO GRAND PRIX SENT THE MOTORSPORTS WORLD INTO SHOCK AND MOURNING.

6. WHICH FORMULA ONE DRIVER BECAME THE YOUNGEST WORLD CHAMPION IN HISTORY IN 2010, THEN SUCCESSFULLY DEFENDED HIS TITLE THE NEXT TWO YEARS?

A. Sebastian Vettel

B. Lewis Hamilton

C. Jenson Button

D. Mark Webber

4.

B. Ferrari fans were understandably less than thrilled when Schumacher decided to make a comeback, at age 41, for a new Mercedes team led by Ross Brawn. Schumacher retired again in 2012.

5.

Ayrton Senna. The three-time world champion won 41 Grand Prix events during his famed career.

6.

A. Vettel, from Germany, was just 23 when he took the Formula One world by storm in 2010.

7. WHERE IS THE INTERNATIONAL
MOTORSPORTS HALL OF FAME LOCATED?

A. Daytona Beach, FL

B. Indianapolis, IN

C. Talladega, AL

D. Bristol, CT

8. THE MOST FAMOUS ENDURANCE RACE IN
THE WORLD, WHICH EVENT CELEBRATED ITS
90TH ANNIVERSARY IN 2013?

9. WHO WAS THE FIRST DRIVER TO WIN THE
DAYTONA 500, INDY 500, 24 HOURS OF
DAYTONA, AND 24 HOURS OF LE MANS?

A. Richard Petty

B. Mario Andretti

C. Dale Earnhardt

D. A.J. Foyt

10. WHAT DISTINCTION DID THE AUDI R18
E-TRON QUATTRO EARN BY WINNING THE
2012 EDITION OF THE 24 HOURS OF LE
MANS?

AUTO RACING

QUESTIONS

7.

C. The IMHOF was founded by NASCAR architect Bill France Sr. near Talladega Superspeedway in 1982.

8.

The 24 Hours of Le Mans. The first running of the "24 Heures du Mans" took place in 1923.

9.

D. Foyt was also the first driver to win the Indy 500 in both a front-engine and rear-engine car.

10.

It became the first hybrid to win the event.

11. NICKNAMED "THE BRICKYARD," WHICH TRACK IS THE WORLD'S LARGEST SPECTATOR SPORTS FACILITY, CONTAINING MORE THAN 250,000 PERMANENT SEATS?

A. Talladega Superspeedway

B. Indianapolis Motor Speedway

C. Daytona International Speedway

D. Richmond International Raceway

12. TRUE OR FALSE?

Danica Patrick was the first woman to race in the Indianapolis 500.

13. WHICH OF THE FOLLOWING DRIVERS DID *NOT* WIN THE INDIANAPOLIS 500 FOUR TIMES?

A. Mario Andretti

B. A.J. Foyt

C. Rick Mears

D. Al Unser Sr.

11.

B. The Indianapolis Motor Speedway, home of the Indianapolis 500, holds that distinction among sports venues. The 253 acres within its oval could house the Roman Colosseum, Churchill Downs, Yankee Stadium, Rose Bowl Stadium, and Vatican City.

12.

False. Janet Guthrie, in 1977, was the first woman to qualify for and race in the Indy 500. Mechanical problems led to an early exit from that race, but the following year she finished ninth—the highest finish for a woman in the Indy 500 until Patrick finished fourth in 2005.

13.

A. For all his many other accomplishments, Andretti won the Indy 500 just once. The others listed share the record with four Indy 500 victories.

14. WHAT BEVERAGE DOES THE WINNER OF THE INDY 500 TRADITIONALLY DRINK IN VICTORY LANE?

15. NAME THE DRIVER WHO, IN 2001 AND '02, BECAME THE FIRST TO WIN THE INDY 500 IN HIS FIRST TWO STARTS.

A. Dan Wheldon

B. Juan Pablo Montoya

C. Helio Castroneves

D. Scott Dixon

16. WHAT LATE TWO-TIME INDY 500 CHAMPION, KILLED IN AN OCTOBER 2011 CRASH IN LAS VEGAS, WAS HONORED WITH A MEMORIAL AND A STREET NAMED AFTER HIM BEFORE THE 2013 ST. PETERSBURG GRAND PRIX?

17. WHICH FORMULA ONE DRIVER, DURING THE 1990S AND 2000S, BROKE JUAN MANUEL FANGIO'S RECORD OF FIVE WORLD CHAMPIONSHIPS?

14.

Milk. After three-time winner Louis Meyer drank buttermilk in victory lane in 1936, a dairy-industry executive made a pitch to keep the tradition going and it caught on.

15.

C. Castroneves was the first to take the checkered flag in his first two Indy 500 starts, and he very nearly became the first driver ever to win three in a row in 2003, when he finished 0.299 seconds behind teammate Gil de Ferran.

16.

Dan Wheldon. The Englishman had made his home in the Florida city after joining the IndyCar circuit.

17.

Michael Schumacher. The German star shattered virtually every Formula One scoring record en route to winning an unprecedented seven world championships.

18. **WHAT ENGINE WON EVERY INDIANAPOLIS 500 BETWEEN 2004 AND '12?**

A. Ford

B. Honda

C. Oldsmobile

D. Chevrolet

19. **WHAT DOES NHRA STAND FOR?**

20. **WHAT MIDWESTERN CITY HAS HOSTED THE ALL-AMERICAN SOAP BOX DERBY SINCE THE 1930S, ATTRACTING YOUNG RACERS FROM ALL OVER THE WORLD?**

A. Akron, OH

B. Dayton, OH

C. Pittsburgh, PA

D. Chicago, IL

18.

B. From Buddy Rice's victory in 2004 to Dario Franchitti's third Indy 500 win in '12, Honda provided the victorious engine.

19.

The National Hot Rod Association, which oversees top-level drag racing in the United States, bills itself as the largest motorsports governing body in the world.

20.

A. Youngsters between the ages of 7 and 17 have been racing at the annual summer festival in Akron since 1935. The first annual event took place in Dayton in 1934, but moved to Akron the following year.

CHASE FOR THE CHECKERS

1. WHAT DOES NASCAR STAND FOR?

2. IN WHAT DECADE WAS NASCAR BORN?

    A. 1930s

    B. 1940s

    C. 1950s

    D. 1960s

3. WHICH INAUGURAL MEMBER OF THE NASCAR HALL OF FAME DIED FOLLOWING A CRASH DURING THE 2001 DAYTONA 500, ENDING A BRILLIANT CAREER IN WHICH HE WON SEVEN CUP CHAMPIONSHIPS?

4. WHAT NUMBER CAR DID DALE EARNHARDT SR. DRIVE?

    A. 3

    B. 5

    C. 8

    D. 44

1.

National Association for Stock Car Auto Racing

2.

B. NASCAR's founding meeting was organized by Bill France Sr. on December 14, 1947, at the Streamline Hotel in Daytona Beach. The circuit, called the "Strictly Stock" division, debuted two years later.

3.

Dale Earnhardt Sr. "The Intimidator," who won back-to-back championships three times in his career, died at age 49.

4.

A. Dale Earnhardt Sr. made the no. 3 Chevrolet famous.

5. **WITH HIS SEVEN POINTS TITLES, WHICH NASCAR LEGEND DID DALE EARNHARDT TIE FOR THE ALL-TIME RECORD?**

A. Darrell Waltrip

B. Cale Yarborough

C. Benny Parsons

D. Richard Petty

6. **TRUE OR FALSE?**

Dale Earnhardt Sr. won the Daytona 500 more times than Richard Petty.

7. **WHICH OF THE FOLLOWING DRIVERS DID *NOT* HAVE A DIRECT RELATIVE WIN THE DAYTONA 500?**

A. Richard Petty

B. Dale Earnhardt Sr.

C. Jamie McMurray

D. Darrell Waltrip

8. **TRUE OR FALSE?**

Jeff Gordon was the first NASCAR driver to host NBC's *Saturday Night Live*.

19

5.

D. "The King," Richard Petty, won seven series titles between 1964 and '79.

6.

False. The Daytona 500 was, for a long time, an elusive goal for Earnhardt. He finally won it in 1998. Petty, on the other hand, dominated NASCAR's signature race with seven victories.

7.

C. Richard Petty's father, Lee, won Daytona, as did Dale Earnhardt Jr. and Darrell Waltrip's brother, Michael. Jamie McMurray is the only member of his family to have won the Daytona 500.

8.

True. He hosted the show in 2003.

9. HOW MANY CONSECUTIVE RACES DID RICHARD PETTY WIN IN 1967, SETTING A NASCAR RECORD THAT MIGHT NEVER BE BROKEN?

A. Seven

B. Eight

C. Nine

D. Ten

10. WHO, IN 2013, BECAME THE FIRST WOMAN EVER TO WIN THE POLE FOR THE DAYTONA 500?

11. NAME THE DRIVER WHO WON NASCAR'S TOP SERIES FIVE YEARS IN A ROW FROM 2006 TO '10.

A. Jeff Gordon

B. Jimmie Johnson

C. Matt Kenseth

D. Tony Stewart

9.

D. On his way to winning 27 of his 48 starts that year, Petty won a remarkable ten in a row. He went on to win 200 races in his career, another record.

10.

Danica Patrick. That's right, the woman who broke barriers with her fourth-place Indy 500 finish in 2005 also made NASCAR history after taking on stock car racing.

11.

B. Johnson was a model of consistency during a stretch in which he became the only driver in history to win five consecutive Cup crowns.

12. WHICH POPULAR **NASCAR** DRIVER WAS THE FASTEST IN HISTORY TO REACH 50 CAREER WINS WHEN HE TOOK THE DieHard 500 AT Talladega IN 2000?

A. Jeff Gordon

B. Tony Stewart

C. Jimmie Johnson

D. Michael Waltrip

13. WHICH OF THE FOLLOWING TRACKS REQUIRES **NASCAR** DRIVERS TO RUN WITH RESTRICTOR PLATES, LIMITING THE SPEED OF THEIR CARS?

A. Bristol

B. Talladega

C. Martinsville

D. Las Vegas

14. WHAT'S THE NAME OF THE BIG **NASCAR** RACE HELD EACH YEAR AT THE INDIANAPOLIS MOTOR SPEEDWAY?

12.

A. Gordon's 50th win came in his 232nd race—46 races fewer than Darrell Waltrip's previous record.

13.

B. Talladega, like Daytona, instituted restrictor-plate requirements largely due to the blazing speeds drivers can achieve on the long straightaways.

14.

The Brickyard 400 brought NASCAR to the Indianapolis Motor Speedway, beginning in 1994.

15. **WHICH THIRD-GENERATION RACER WAS VOTED BY FANS NASCAR'S MOST POPULAR DRIVER 10 YEARS IN A ROW?**

A. Jeff Gordon

B. Jimmie Johnson

C. Dale Earnhardt Jr.

D. Kurt Busch

16. **NAME THE 28-YEAR-OLD 2012 CUP CHAMPION WHO ENDEARED HIMSELF TO YOUNGER FANS BY "TWEETING" (SENDING A TWITTER UPDATE) DURING A RED FLAG AT THAT YEAR'S DAYTONA 500.**

A. Greg Biffle

B. Clint Bowyer

C. Carl Edwards

D. Brad Keselowski

17. **WHAT ACROBATIC MANEUVER DOES CARL EDWARDS ROUTINELY PERFORM AFTER A VICTORY?**

15.

C. Dale Jr. joined Bill Elliott as the only drivers to win the award every year for a decade.

16.

D. Keselowski became just the third under-30 driver since 1985 to win a Cup title.

17.

A backflip is Edwards' signature celebration.

18. WHICH AUTO MANUFACTURER HAS WON THE MOST CUP TITLES IN NASCAR?

A. Ford

B. Chevrolet

C. Dodge

D. Buick

19. NASCAR INSTALLED A PLAYOFF-LIKE FORMAT IN 2004 TO INCREASE EXCITEMENT OVER ITS ANNUAL POINTS TITLE. WHAT IS THAT "PLAYOFF" CALLED?

20. TRUE OR FALSE?

There was a tie in the NASCAR series points standings in 2011, requiring a tie-breaker to determine the Cup champion.

18.

B. Chevy, by far, has the most titles. Its 2012 crown with Brad Keselowski was its 10th in a row and 36th overall.

19.

The Chase, or the Chase for the Cup. It gives the top drivers during the season a chance to compete for the overall championship.

20.

True. Tony Stewart and Carl Edwards were dead even in the final points. Stewart won his third Cup title based on total wins during the year.

BASEBALL

REGULAR SEASON

1. **WHICH MEMBER OF THE 3,000-HIT CLUB WAS THE FIRST TO REACH THAT MILESTONE ON A HOME RUN?**

A. Derek Jeter

B. Wade Boggs

C. Paul Molitor

D. Pete Rose

2. **TRUE OR FALSE?**

Cincinnati's longstanding tradition of playing at home on Opening Day stems from the fact the Reds (then the Red Stockings) were the Major Leagues' first team in 1869.

1.

B. While Jeter did homer for his 3,000th hit in 2011, Boggs did it 12 years earlier for his hometown team, Tampa Bay. Molitor, incidentally, was the first man to triple for his 3,000th hit.

2.

False. While the Reds were the originals, the honor of starting the season at home—an honor the city celebrates with an annual parade—is due more to geography than anything else. The weather in southern Ohio is typically better in April than it is in locales to the north.

3. **WHEN ADAM DUNN HIT HIS EIGHTH CAREER OPENING DAY HOME RUN IN 2013, WHOSE MAJOR LEAGUE RECORD DID HE MATCH?**

4. **THROWING ONE NO-HITTER IS TOUGH ENOUGH, BUT WHICH MAJOR LEAGUE PITCHER TOSSED BACK-TO-BACK NO-HITTERS IN 1938?**

    A. Carl Hubbell

    B. Hoyt Wilhelm

    C. Johnny Vander Meer

    D. Lefty Gomez

5. **WHY DO THE OAKLAND ATHLETICS HAVE AN ELEPHANT AS THEIR MASCOT?**

    A. Their affiliation with the Republican party

    B. An original owner co-wrote Walt Disney's *Dumbo*

    C. Because an elephant is said to "never forget"

    D. To spite a former opposing manager

3.

Frank Robinson and Ken Griffey Jr. each hit eight Opening Day homers.

4.

C. Vander Meer, a Cincinnati Reds left-hander, no-hit the Boston Braves and Brooklyn Dodgers in consecutive games. His unprecedented second straight "no-no," on June 15 at Ebbets Field, was also the first night baseball game in New York City.

5.

D. In 1902, New York Giants manager John McGraw dismissed the Philadelphia Athletics, calling them "White Elephants" with contempt. Athletics boss Connie Mack defiantly made the elephant his team's insignia, and it stuck.

6. WHICH SLUGGER, IN 2012, BECAME THE FIRST PLAYER IN HISTORY TO HIT AT LEAST 30 HOME RUNS IN EACH OF HIS FIRST 12 MAJOR LEAGUE SEASONS?

A. Albert Pujols

B. Alex Rodriguez

C. Prince Fielder

D. Adrian Beltre

7. TED WILLIAMS REFUSED TO SIT OUT A DOUBLEHEADER ON THE FINAL DAY OF THE 1941 SEASON TO PRESERVE A .400 BATTING AVERAGE. HOW MANY HITS DID HE COLLECT AGAINST THE PHILADELPHIA ATHLETICS THAT DAY?

8. WHO WAS THE FIRST PLAYER TO WIN THE MVP AWARD IN BOTH THE NATIONAL AND AMERICAN LEAGUES?

6.

A. Pujols joined Rodriguez, Barry Bonds, and Jimmie Foxx in hitting 30 or more homers in 12 straight seasons, but none of the others did it in his first 12.

7.

Six. Williams went 6-for-8 to finish the season with a .406 average.

8.

Frank Robinson won the NL MVP Award with the Cincinnati Reds in 1961 and AL MVP honors with the Baltimore Orioles in '66.

9. THE DOMINICAN REPUBLIC WON THE 2012 WORLD BASEBALL CLASSIC, BUT WHICH COUNTRY CAPTURED THE FIRST TWO EDITIONS OF THE EVENT IN '06 AND '09?

A. USA

B. Canada

C. Japan

D. Cuba

10. TRUE OR FALSE?

The National League once won 11 consecutive Major League All-Star Games against the American League.

11. WHICH OF THE FOLLOWING IS NOT A PART OF WRIGLEY FIELD'S STORIED HISTORY?

A. It was once called Weeghman Park.

B. A flag bearing a "W" or "L" flies above the field after each Chicago Cubs game.

C. It opened its gates for the 1912 season.

D. Lights were added in 1988.

9.

C. Japan defeated Cuba in the inaugural World Baseball Classic in '06 and South Korea in '09. Both times, pitcher Daisuke Matsuzaka earned MVP honors.

10.

True. The longest winning streak in All-Star Game history began in Atlanta in 1972 and was not broken until the AL prevailed at Chicago's Comiskey Park in 1983. Throw in another eight-game winning streak in the '60s, and the NL actually defeated the AL 19 times in 20 years.

11.

C. Wrigley, then called Weeghman Park, hosted its first game April 23, 1914. It was Boston's Fenway Park that opened in 1912.

12. WHO WAS THE FIRST PLAYER IN MAJOR LEAGUE HISTORY TO HIT 30 HOME RUNS, STEAL 45 BASES, AND SCORE 125 RUNS IN A SINGLE SEASON?

A. Albert Pujols

B. Jackie Robinson

C. Barry Bonds

D. Mike Trout

13. MIGUEL CABRERA OF THE DETROIT TIGERS WON THE AMERICAN LEAGUE TRIPLE CROWN IN 2012, LEADING THE LEAGUE IN BATTING, HOME RUNS, AND RBI. BEFORE "MIGGY," WHO WAS THE LAST TRIPLE CROWN WINNER?

A. Jim Rice

B. George Brett

C. Carl Yastrzemski

D. Mickey Mantle

12.

D. Trout made history during 2012, and he did most of the damage before celebrating his 21st birthday. His unprecedented season earned the Los Angeles Angels star the 2012 AL Rookie of the Year Award.

13.

C. "Yaz" treated Boston Red Sox fans to a Triple Crown in 1967. It would be the last one in the Majors for 45 years before Cabrera came along.

14. **WHICH HALL OF FAMER APPEARS ON THE MOST VALUABLE BASEBALL CARD IN THE WORLD?**

A. Babe Ruth

B. Honus Wagner

C. Ted Williams

D. Ty Cobb

15. **TRUE OR FALSE?**

Brothers B.J. and Justin Upton hit their 100th career Major League home runs on the exact same day in 2012.

16. **A WHOPPING SEVEN NO-HITTERS WERE THROWN DURING THE 2012 SEASON. WHEN WAS THE LAST TIME THERE WERE THAT MANY NO-NO'S IN A YEAR?**

A. 1991

B. 1981

C. 1971

D. 1961

14.

B. The 1909 Honus Wagner T-206 card, because of its scarcity, has for many years been the most valuable card on the market. One sold in 2013 for more than $2 million.

15.

True. B.J. reached the century mark on August 3, and 44 minutes later younger brother Justin hit his 100th, too. Of the five previous brother tandems to compile 100 career home runs, none ever hit homers on the same day.

16.

A. There were also seven in 1991, including Nolan Ryan's record seventh (and final) one.

17. WHO WAS THE FIRST PITCHER IN MAJOR
LEAGUE HISTORY TO LOSE A NO-HITTER?

A. Sandy Koufax

B. Ken Johnson

C. Whitey Ford

D. Nolan Ryan

18. WHICH MASTER OF THE CUT FASTBALL SET
THE MAJOR LEAGUE RECORD FOR CAREER
SAVES IN 2011?

19. WHICH OF THE FOLLOWING WAS *NOT* A
PUBLIC-RELATIONS STUNT DESIGNED BY
THE WACKY BILL VEECK?

A. Sending 3'7" Eddie Gaedel to the plate

B. Allowing fans to make managerial decisions via
cue cards

C. Putting a golf driver in a struggling player's
hands

D. Disco Demolition Night in Chicago

20. WHICH FORMER NATIONAL LEAGUE TEAM
MOVED TO THE AMERICAN LEAGUE IN 2013?

17.

B. Johnson, pitching for the Houston Colt .45s, threw a no-hitter against the Cincinnati Reds on April 24, 1964, but suffered a 1–0 defeat. Johnson threw wildly to first base on Pete Rose's bunt in the ninth inning, and a subsequent error by second baseman Nellie Fox allowed the winning run to cross.

18.

Mariano Rivera, routinely throwing nothing but "cutters," broke Trevor Hoffman's mark when he notched his 602nd career save.

19.

C. Veeck made a career out of wacky promotions, but a golf club was not among his many stunts.

20.

The Houston Astros. After 51 years in the NL, the Astros made the unprecedented move to the AL to begin the 2013 season.

21. THE LOS ANGELES DODGERS AND BOSTON RED SOX PLAYED A 2008 EXHIBITION AT THE LOS ANGELES COLISEUM THAT DREW A RECORD CROWD FOR A PRO BASEBALL GAME. HOW MANY PEOPLE ATTENDED?

A. 95,300

B. 105,300

C. 115,300

D. 125,300

22. WHICH HITTING MACHINE BROKE GEORGE SISLER'S 84-YEAR-OLD MAJOR LEAGUE RECORD FOR HITS IN A SEASON DURING 2004?

23. TRUE OR FALSE?

Despite batting .406 in 1941, Ted Williams did not win the American League MVP Award that year.

21.

C. The 115,300 fans broke—by about a thousand—the previous record set at the 1956 Melbourne Olympics in Australia.

22.

Ichiro Suzuki. The Seattle Mariners star rapped 259 hits, two more than Sisler had way back in 1920.

23.

True. That was also the year Joe DiMaggio hit in a Major League record 56 consecutive games, and the New York Yankees star took MVP honors.

24. SINCE JOE DIMAGGIO SET THE MAJOR LEAGUE RECORD WITH A 56-GAME HITTING STREAK IN 1941, WHO WAS THE FIRST PLAYER TO CRACK THE 40-GAME MARK IN PURSUIT?

A. Pete Rose

B. Ichiro Suzuki

C. Rod Carew

D. Wade Boggs

25. BARRY BONDS BROKE THREE MAJOR LEAGUE RECORDS THAT HAD STOOD FOR MORE THAN 60 YEARS. WHICH WAS NOT ONE OF THEM?

A. On-base percentage in a season

B. Bases on balls in a season

C. Career bases on balls

D. Slugging percentage in a season

26. CAL RIPKEN JR. DID WHAT, EXACTLY, OVER A STRING OF A RECORD 2,362 CONSECUTIVE GAMES?

BASEBALL

24.

A. Rose put together a 44-game hitting streak in 1978.

25.

C. Bonds broke the three longstanding single-season records mentioned, but it was Ricky Henderson who broke Babe Ruth's 66-year-old career record for walks.

26.

Played. The Baltimore Orioles star broke Lou Gehrig's longstanding "Iron Man" record between 1983 and '98, never missing a game.

27. WHO HOLDS THE MAJOR LEAGUE RECORD FOR CAREER BATTING AVERAGE?

A. Rogers Hornsby

B. Ty Cobb

C. "Shoeless" Joe Jackson

D. Tris Speaker

28. NAME THE PITCHER WHO BROKE HIS CLUB'S SINGLE-GAME STRIKEOUT RECORD WITH 14 IN HIS MAJOR LEAGUE DEBUT ON JUNE 8, 2010.

29. JACKIE ROBINSON BROKE BASEBALL'S COLOR BARRIER IN 1947 AND WENT ON TO LEAD THE NATIONAL LEAGUE IN SEVERAL CATEGORIES DURING HIS CAREER. WHICH WAS *NOT* ONE OF THEM?

A. Batting

B. On-base percentage

C. Stolen bases

D. Runs

27.

B. Cobb's .366 career average is eight points better than any other in history.

28.

Stephen Strasburg. The highly-touted youngster—just 21 at the time—set the Washington Nationals record over seven innings of a 5–2 win over the Pittsburgh Pirates.

29.

D. While Robinson scored 100 or more runs in a season six different times, he never led the NL in that category.

30. WHICH NATIONAL LEAGUER BECAME THE YOUNGEST PLAYER IN MAJOR LEAGUE HISTORY TO BELT TWO HOME RUNS ON OPENING DAY WHEN HE DID SO IN 2013?

A. Buster Posey

B. Bryce Harper

C. David Wright

D. Joey Votto

31. RICKEY HENDERSON LED THE MAJOR LEAGUES IN THREE CATEGORIES IN 1982. WHICH WAS NOT ONE OF THEM?

A. Doubles

B. Bases on balls

C. Stolen bases

D. Caught stealing

32. TRUE OR FALSE?

Theo Epstein was both the youngest general manager in Major League history and the youngest GM to win a World Series title.

30.

B. Harper, of the Washington Nationals, was just 20 when he went deep twice to power a 2–0 Opening Day win over Miami.

31.

A. Henderson walked 116 times, stole a Major League-record 130 bases and was caught stealing 42 times—all Major League highs that season.

32.

True. Epstein, then with the Boston Red Sox, was just 28 when he was hired in 2002 and became the youngest GM to win a championship two years later.

33. WHICH LOS ANGELES DODGERS PITCHER SET A RECORD IN 1988 WITH 59 CONSECUTIVE SCORELESS INNINGS?

34. WHY DID FANS IN MILWAUKEE CHANT "LET THEM PLAY!" AFTER THE 11TH INNING OF THE 2002 ALL-STAR GAME?

A. Because of a long rain delay

B. Because of a prolonged power outage

C. Because they didn't want the game to end in a tie

D. Because visiting Little Leaguers wanted to play another inning

35. WHAT RULE CHANGE CELEBRATED ITS 40TH ANNIVERSARY IN 2013?

A. Ground-rule double

B. Designated hitter rule

C. Raised pitcher's mound

D. Mandatory batting helmets

33.

Orel Hershiser. The streak featured an amazing five consecutive scoreless shutouts, including two on three days' rest.

34.

C. A decision was made by the managers and Commissioner Bud Selig to end the game after the 11th inning with the score tied 7–7, since both teams had exhausted their pitching options. It was not a popular decision among fans.

35.

B. The American League adopted the designated hitter in 1973.

WORLD SERIES

1. WHAT LAST NAME WOULD YOU SHOUT IF YOU WERE TRYING TO GET THE ATTENTION OF THE FIRST TRIO OF BROTHERS EVER TO WIN WORLD SERIES TITLES?

2. WHICH MANAGER WAS THE FIRST TO WIN WORLD SERIES TITLES IN BOTH LEAGUES?

3. WHO HOLDS THE RECORD FOR MOST CAREER HOME RUNS IN WORLD SERIES PLAY?

    A. Babe Ruth

    B. Mickey Mantle

    C. Duke Snider

    D. Yogi Berra

4. BEFORE THE SAN FRANCISCO GIANTS SWEPT THE DETROIT TIGERS IN FOUR GAMES TO WIN THE 2012 WORLD SERIES, WHEN WAS THE LAST TIME A NATIONAL LEAGUE TEAM RECORDED A WORLD SERIES SWEEP?

1.

Molina! Bengie, the oldest, and Jose won champion-ships as Los Angeles Angels teammates in 2002, and younger brother Yadier joined the club with the St. Louis Cardinals in 2006 and '11—all as catchers. Jose added another to the family trophy case as a New York Yankee in '09.

2.

Sparky Anderson captured his first two World Series championships at the Cincinnati Reds (NL) helm in 1975 and '76, and then took the Detroit Tigers (AL) to the top in '84. He was also the first manager to enjoy 100-win seasons in both leagues.

3.

B. Mantle, with 18 World Series home runs, topped Babe Ruth's previous record by three.

4.

1990. That's when the Cincinnati Reds took four straight over the Oakland Athletics.

5. WHICH OF THESE WORLD SERIES MVPS DID *NOT* EARN THE HONOR AS A CATCHER?

A. Pat Borders

B. Steve Yeager

C. Ray Knight

D. Gene Tenace

6. WHAT NICKNAME DID REGGIE JACKSON EARN, IN PART, BY HITTING HOME RUNS ON FOUR STRAIGHT SWINGS OF THE BAT IN THE 1977 WORLD SERIES?

A. Mr. October

B. The Series Slugger

C. Straw that Stirs the Drink

D. Rockin' Reggie

7. WHICH PITCHER, IN 2010, THREW THE FIRST POSTSEASON NO-HITTER SINCE DON LARSEN'S PERFECT GAME IN THE 1956 WORLD SERIES?

5.

C. Knight played third base for the New York Mets when he won World Series MVP honors in 1986.

6.

A. The New York Yankees slugger came to be known as Mr. October for the postseason damage he did with the bat.

7.

Roy Halladay. Making his postseason debut, the Philadelphia Phillies ace no-hit the Cincinnati Reds in Game 1 of the National League Division Series.

8. WHEN HE WASN'T BUTCHERING THE
ENGLISH LANGUAGE WITH HIS UNIQUE
WIT, YOGI BERRA COULD FREQUENTLY BE
FOUND PLAYING IN THE WORLD SERIES.
HOW MANY TIMES DID THE LONGTIME NEW
YORK YANKEES CATCHER REACH THE FALL
CLASSIC?

A. 11

B. 12

C. 13

D. 14

9. WHICH PLAYER, IN 2000, BECAME THE FIRST
IN MAJOR LEAGUE HISTORY NAMED MVP
OF BOTH THE ALL-STAR GAME AND WORLD
SERIES IN THE SAME YEAR?

A. Derek Jeter

B. Mariano Rivera

C. Roger Clemens

D. Alex Rodriguez

8.

D. Berra played in the World Series a record 14 times.

9.

A. Jeter accomplished the feat after going 9-for-22 with two home runs to lead the New York Yankees to a five-game World Series win over the New York Mets. He went 3-for-3 with two RBI in the All-Star Game.

10. TRUE OR FALSE?

"Shoeless" Joe Jackson went 12-for-32 (.375) during the 1919 World Series—the one for which he and seven Chicago White Sox teammates were banned for life for their roles in "fixing" games.

11. IN WHAT YEAR DID THE PHILADELPHIA PHILLIES WIN THEIR FIRST WORLD SERIES?

A. 1960

B. 1970

C. 1980

D. 1990

12. WHEN DID MAJOR LEAGUE BASEBALL FIRST ALLOW "WILD CARD" TEAMS INTO THE PLAYOFFS?

A. 2000

B. 1994

C. 1987

D. 1982

10.

True. For someone who was allegedly trying to "throw" games, Jackson's 12 hits still stand as a record for an eight-game World Series (before the format changed to best-of-seven).

11.

C. Although they reached the World Series in 1915 and 1950, the Philadelphia Phillies won it all for the first time in 1980.

12.

B. Expansion to three divisions per year in 1994 paved the way for "wild card" playoff entries. However, due to a strike that season, the first such entries did not see postseason action until the following year.

ON CAMPUS

1. WHICH COACH, IN 2013, BECAME THE FIRST EVER TO LEAD TWO DIFFERENT SCHOOLS TO MEN'S NCAA DIVISION I CHAMPIONSHIPS?

A. Steve Alford

B. John Beilein

C. Jim Boeheim

D. Rick Pitino

2. WHO WAS KNOWN AS THE "WIZARD OF WESTWOOD"?

A. John Wooden

B. Woody Hayes

C. Sean Woods

D. Bobby Knight

1.

D. On the same day he learned he would be inducted into the Basketball Hall of Fame, Pitino coached Louisville past Michigan for the national title. He had taken Kentucky all the way 17 years earlier, making him the first coach ever to win titles at two different Division I schools.

2.

A. The legendary John Wooden came to be known by this nickname while coaching UCLA to college basketball greatness.

3. WHICH CAME FIRST IN MEN'S COLLEGE BASKETBALL—THE SHOT CLOCK OR THE 3-POINT LINE?

4. HOW MANY NATIONAL CHAMPIONSHIPS DID UCLA WIN IN THE JOHN WOODEN COACHING ERA?

A. Seven

B. Eight

C. Nine

D. Ten

5. TRUE OR FALSE?

It was North Carolina that ended UCLA's record 88-game winning streak in 1974.

6. WHO IS THE ONLY PLAYER EVER NAMED NCAA FINAL FOUR MVP THREE TIMES?

A. Bill Walton

B. Elvin Hayes

C. Lewis Alcindor

D. Michael Jordan

3.

The shot clock was first, by one year. A 45-second shot clock was added in 1985-86 in an effort to increase scoring. The 3-point arc debuted in 1986-87.

4.

D. The Bruins won ten national titles under Wooden between 1963 and '75.

5.

False. It was Notre Dame. In fact, the Bruins' last loss before starting their amazing streak in '71 was also to the Fighting Irish.

6.

C. Lewis Alcindor, before he became known as Kareem Abdul-Jabbar, was honored as MVP in 1967, '68, and '69.

7. WHO MADE THE WINNING SHOT IN NORTH CAROLINA'S 1982 NCAA TITLE GAME VICTORY OVER GEORGETOWN?

A. Michael Jordan

B. James Worthy

C. Jimmy Black

D. Phil Ford

8. WHAT WAS THE NAME OF THE FICTITIOUS "FRATERNITY" BY WHICH THE HOUSTON COUGARS OF CLYDE DREXLER AND HAKEEM (THEN AKEEM) OLAJUWON WERE KNOWN IN THE EARLY 1980S?

9. WHICH OF THE FOLLOWING SCHOOLS DID *NOT* CAPTURE *TWO* NCAA MEN'S BASKETBALL CHAMPIONSHIPS BETWEEN 2001 AND '10?

A. Florida

B. Kansas

C. North Carolina

D. Duke

7.

A. Jordan, just a freshman at the time, launched a long career of clutch shooting and winning championships when his 17-footer led the Tar Heels to victory.

8.

Phi Slamma Jamma

9.

B. Kansas won one title during the decade (2008), while the rest won two apiece.

10. **WHICH BASKETBALL POWER WAS THE FIRST TO CAPTURE BACK-TO-BACK TITLES SINCE UCLA WON SEVEN NATIONAL CHAMPIONSHIPS IN A ROW IN THE 1960S AND '70S?**

A. Duke

B. North Carolina

C. N.C. State

D. UNLV

11. **TRUE OR FALSE?**

The man Duke coach Mike Krzyzewski passed to become the winningest coach in major men's college basketball history in 2011 was his friend, mentor and former coach, Bob Knight.

12. **WHICH SCHOOL, IN 2004, BECAME THE FIRST TO CLAIM BOTH THE MEN'S AND WOMEN'S NCAA DIVISION I BASKETBALL CHAMPIONSHIPS IN THE SAME YEAR?**

67

10.

A. Duke won consecutive crowns in 1991 and '92.

11.

True. "Coach K" played for Knight at West Point (Army) and later served as a graduate assistant under Knight at Indiana University.

12.

Connecticut. The Huskies defeated Georgia Tech in the men's final, and the next day the UConn women knocked off Tennessee to double the fun.

13. PRESIDENT BILL CLINTON WAS IN THE
CROWD FOR THE 1994 NCAA MEN'S
BASKETBALL TITLE GAME, CHEERING ON
WHICH TEAM TO A VICTORY OVER DUKE?

A. Kansas

B. North Carolina

C. Arkansas

D. UNLV

14. WHEN CONNECTICUT COACH GENO
AURIEMMA WON HIS EIGHTH NCAA
WOMEN'S BASKETBALL CHAMPIONSHIP IN
2013, WHICH LEGENDARY COACH DID HE
TIE FOR MOST WOMEN'S TITLES?

A. Vivian Stringer

B. Pat Summitt

C. Tara VanDerveer

D. Kay Yow

13.

C. Clinton, an Arkansas native and former governor of the state, was also on hand for the Razorbacks' regional final victory against Michigan that year, becoming the first sitting president to attend an NCAA tournament game.

14.

B. Summitt won eight national titles during her tenure at Tennessee from 1974 to 2012.

15. WHICH OF THE FOLLOWING PLAYERS WAS *NOT* A MEMBER OF MICHIGAN'S FAMED "FAB FIVE" CLASS OF THE EARLY 1990s?

A. Jalen Rose

B. Jimmy King

C. Rumeal Robinson

D. Chris Webber

16. TRUE OR FALSE?

An official NCAA women's basketball is smaller than a men's ball.

17. WHICH OF THE FOLLOWING COACHES DID *NOT* HAVE AN ARENA NAMED IN HIS HONOR?

A. Bob Knight

B. Dean Smith

C. "Phog" Allen

D. Adolph Rupp

15.

C. Robinson was the hero of Michigan's 1989 NCAA championship, hitting two free throws in OT to beat Seton Hall, but that was before the arrival of the "Fab Five."

16.

True. The men's ball has a 30-inch maximum circumference; the women's ball has a 29-inch maximum circumference.

17.

A. North Carolina calls the Dean Smith Center home, Kentucky is tough to beat at Rupp Arena, and Kansas plays at Allen Fieldhouse. Despite Knight's success, particularly at Indiana, his name does not grace the Hoosiers' home court.

18. **UNDER DON HASKINS IN 1966, TEXAS WESTERN COLLEGE UPSET KENTUCKY TO BECOME THE FIRST NCAA MEN'S BASKETBALL CHAMPION WITH AN ALL-BLACK STARTING LINEUP. WHAT SCHOOL DID TEXAS WESTERN BECOME?**

A. Texas Christian

B. Texas-El Paso

C. Texas A&M

D. Texas State

19. **WHO FIRED THE MOST EFFECTIVE "AIRBALL" IN COLLEGE BASKETBALL HISTORY (A DESPERATION SHOT THAT N.C. STATE TEAMMATE LORENZO CHARLES GRABBED IN MID-AIR AND DUNKED AT THE BUZZER FOR THE WINNING BASKET IN THE 1983 NCAA CHAMPIONSHIP GAME AGAINST HOUSTON)?**

A. Sidney Lowe

B. Jim Valvano

C. Thurl Bailey

D. Dereck Whittenburg

18.

B. In 1967, Texas Western College became known as the University of Texas at El Paso.

19.

D. Whittenburg put up the shot, though he has insisted for years—with a smile on his face—that it was a well-placed pass.

20. WHICH TWO FUTURE NBA STARS CAPTIVATED COLLEGE BASKETBALL FANS DURING THEIR BATTLE FOR THE 1979 NCAA CHAMPIONSHIP?

21. LATE N.C. STATE COACH JIM VALVANO SPENT MUCH OF HIS CAREER BATTLING ACC RIVALS LIKE DUKE AND NORTH CAROLINA. WHAT DOES HIS JIMMY V FOUNDATION NOW BATTLE?

A. Cancer

B. Leukemia

C. Bullying

D. Cheating in sports

22. WHAT DOES NIT STAND FOR?

20.

Michigan State's Magic Johnson prevailed over Indiana State's Larry Bird in what was then the highest-rated college basketball game in television history.

21.

A. For more than 20 years, the Jimmy V Foundation has been raising money to fight cancer. Its motto comes from a famous speech in which Valvano urged, "Don't give up...don't ever give up."

22.

National Invitation Tournament. Originating in 1938, it predates the NCAA tournament.

GOING PRO

1. THE 2012-13 MIAMI HEAT MADE A VALIANT RUN AT WHICH TEAM'S NBA-RECORD 33-GAME WINNING STREAK?

A. Boston Celtics

B. Los Angeles Lakers

C. Philadelphia 76ers

D. Milwaukee Bucks

2. WHICH OF THE FOLLOWING COACHES WON MORE CAREER NBA GAMES?

A. Pat Riley

B. Lenny Wilkens

C. Don Nelson

D. Bill Fitch

3. TRUE OR FALSE?

LeBron James has won more NBA MVP Awards than any player since 2000.

1.

B. The Miami Heat came within six games of the Los Angeles Lakers' legendary record, set in 1971-72.

2.

C. Nelson, who coached from 1977 to 2010, passed Wilkens atop the career win list, retiring with 1,335.

3.

True. "King James" won his fourth NBA MVP Award after the 2012-13 season, giving him two more than Tim Duncan and Steve Nash since 2000.

4. WHICH POINT GUARD, IN 2011, BECAME THE YOUNGEST PLAYER EVER TO WIN THE NBA MVP AWARD?

A. Kobe Bryant

B. Allen Iverson

C. Jason Kidd

D. Derrick Rose

5. WHICH BIG MAN WON NBA DEFENSIVE PLAYER OF THE YEAR HONORS THREE STRAIGHT TIMES FROM 2009 TO '11?

6. MICHAEL JORDAN LED THE CHICAGO BULLS TO SIX NBA CHAMPIONSHIPS IN THE 1990S. HOW MANY NBA FINALS MVP AWARDS DID HE WIN ALONG THE WAY?

A. Six

B. Five

C. Four

D. Three

4.

D. Rose, just 22, became the first Chicago Bulls player to win MVP honors since Michael Jordan.

5.

Dwight Howard, then playing for the Orlando Magic, was named the NBA's top defender three years in a row.

6.

A. Yes, MJ was MVP of all six of his NBA Finals appearances after leading his team to victory in each.

7. OTHER THAN MICHAEL JORDAN, WHO
CAPTURED MORE THAN ONE NBA FINALS
MVP AWARD IN THE 1990S?

A. Tim Duncan

B. Hakeem Olajuwon

C. Scottie Pippen

D. Isiah Thomas

8. MICHAEL JORDAN TIED AN NBA RECORD BY
WINNING SEVEN CONSECUTIVE SCORING TITLES.
WITH WHOM DOES HE SHARE THAT MARK?

9. TRUE OR FALSE?

With four points, Willis Reed was considered the hero
of the New York Knicks' win in Game 7 of the 1970
NBA Finals.

10. WINNING THREE CONSECUTIVE NBA
CHAMPIONSHIPS—SOMETIMES CALLED
A "THREE-PEAT"—IS AN AMAZING
ACHIEVEMENT. WHICH COACH DID IT
THREE DIFFERENT TIMES, WITH TWO
DIFFERENT TEAMS?

7.

B. In 1994, Olajuwon became the first center since Kareem Abdul-Jabbar to win NBA Finals MVP honors, and he won it again the following year after leading the Houston Rockets to back-to-back titles.

8.

Wilt Chamberlain

9.

True. An injured Reed was not supposed to play against the Los Angeles Lakers and did not participate in warm-ups, but he hobbled onto the court, took the opening tip and scored the first two baskets of the game. His teammates then picked up the scoring and won the first NBA title in team history.

10.

Phil Jackson. Jackson led the Chicago Bulls to three straight titles twice in the 1990s, and then took the Los Angeles Lakers to three straight beginning with the 2000 championship.

11. **WHICH LOS ANGELES LAKER WON THREE CONSECUTIVE NBA FINALS MVP AWARDS FROM 2000 TO '02?**

A. Kobe Bryant

B. Derek Fisher

C. Shaquille O'Neal

D. Horace Grant

12. **WILT CHAMBERLAIN WAS A 51-PERCENT CAREER SHOOTER FROM THE FREE THROW LINE. HOW MANY OF HIS 32 FREE THROW ATTEMPTS DID HE CONVERT DURING HIS NBA RECORD 100-POINT GAME IN 1962?**

A. 12

B. 17

C. 24

D. 28

13. **WHILE WILT CHAMBERLAIN WAS LIGHTING UP SCOREBOARDS, WHICH OF HIS CONTEMPORARIES WAS A DEFENSIVE FORCE PLAYING CENTER FOR A BOSTON CELTICS TEAM THAT WON 11 NBA CHAMPIONSHIPS IN 13 YEARS?**

11.

C. Though Bryant would go on to win NBA Finals MVP honors later in the decade, it was "Shaq" who earned the hardware after his team's three consecutive titles.

12.

D. Talk about coming up big when it counted. Wilt traded his usual bricks for swishes, hitting free throws at an .875 rate during his signature game to lead the Philadelphia Warriors past the New York Knicks, 169-147.

13.

Bill Russell. The big man could score, too, but was known for his defense, rebounding, quickness, intelligence and leadership while leading the NBA's greatest dynasty.

14. **WHICH VERSATILE MILWAUKEE BUCKS LEGEND WON THE FIRST TWO NBA DEFENSIVE PLAYER OF THE YEAR AWARDS IN 1983 AND '84?**

A. Sidney Moncrief

B. Kareem Abdul-Jabbar

C. Marques Johnson

D. Bob Lanier

15. **TRUE OR FALSE?**

Julius Erving is the all-time scoring leader in Philadelphia 76ers history.

16. **BY WHAT NICKNAME WAS THE PHILADELPHIA 76ERS GREAT JULIUS ERVING COMMONLY KNOWN?**

A. Iceman

B. Dr. Dunkenstein

C. Dr. J

D. Ace

14.

A. Moncrief made steals, blocked shots, and forced his matchup to work tirelessly for every look at the basket over 11 NBA seasons—10 with the Milwaukee Bucks.

15.

False. With 18,364 points, Erving is up there. But Hal Greer holds the franchise scoring record with more than 21,000 career points.

16.

C. Dr. J operated at a level unfamiliar to his contemporaries in the 1970s and '80s, bringing an excitement and showmanship to the floor that paved the way for players like Magic Johnson and Michael Jordan.

17. WHICH OF THESE GREATS IS *NOT* IN THE BASKETBALL HALL OF FAME FOR HIS ROLE WITH THE BOSTON CELTICS?

A. Bill Walton

B. Jerry West

C. Bob Cousy

D. Kevin McHale

18. WHY IS A TEAM BASED IN LOS ANGELES NICKNAMED THE LAKERS?

19. WHO STARRED AT CENTER FOR THE LOS ANGELES LAKERS WHEN THEY BEAT THE PHILADELPHIA 76ERS IN GAME 6 TO WIN THE 1980 NBA FINALS?

A. James Worthy

B. Moses Malone

C. Kareem-Abdul Jabbar

D. Magic Johnson

17.

B. While the others are Boston Celtics Hall of Famers, West starred for the rival Los Angeles Lakers.

18.

Because they used to play in Minnesota, the "Land of 10,000 Lakes," before becoming the NBA's first West Coast team before the 1960-61 season. The Minneapolis Lakers featured one of the league's first superstars in George Mikan.

19.

D. Despite the fact he was a point guard, Magic—a rookie at the time—volunteered to play center in the absence of an injured Jabbar. He scored 42 points, made all 14 free throws, grabbed 15 rebounds, and had seven assists and three steals to lead his team to the title.

20. WHICH OF THE FOLLOWING MEMBERS OF THE 1982-83 NBA CHAMPION PHILADELPHIA 76ERS DID *NOT* PLAY IN THE AMERICAN BASKETBALL ASSOCIATION, WHICH DISBANDED IN 1976?

A. Maurice Cheeks

B. Moses Malone

C. Bobby Jones

D. Julius Erving

21. WHAT WAS DISTINCTIVE ABOUT THE BALL USED BY THE ABA?

22. WHICH NBA TEAM GAVE WOMEN'S BASKETBALL GREAT ANN MEYERS A HIGHLY-PUBLICIZED TRYOUT IN 1979?

A. Boston Celtics

B. Phoenix Suns

C. Indiana Pacers

D. Detroit Pistons

20.

A. Cheeks played pro ball only in the NBA. The other three—comprising one heck of a frontcourt—were all former ABA standouts.

21.

It was red, white, and blue. The ABA was also the first pro league to allow teenagers to play, and the first to adopt the 3-point shot.

22.

C. Meyers tried out for the Indiana Pacers but did not make the team. She went on to a successful career in broadcasting.

23. WHICH NBA TEAM WAS THE FIRST TO WIN AT LEAST 70 GAMES IN A SEASON?

A. 1964-65 Boston Celtics

B. 1969-70 New York Knicks

C. 1986-87 Los Angeles Lakers

D. 1995-96 Chicago Bulls

24. WHO, OVER 19 SEASONS WITH THE UTAH JAZZ, BECAME THE NBA'S CAREER LEADER IN ASSISTS?

A. Karl Malone

B. Moses Malone

C. John Stockton

D. Jason Kidd

25. NAME THE NBA'S CAREER SCORING LEADER.

A. Michael Jordan

B. Kareem Abdul-Jabbar

C. Wilt Chamberlain

D. Karl Malone

91

23.

D. Michael Jordan, Scottie Pippen, and the 1995–96 Chicago Bulls compiled a remarkable 72–10 record, becoming the first NBA team to win 70 in a season. They started the year 41–3.

24.

C. In addition to becoming the all-time NBA assists leader, Stockton also set the career record for assists.

25.

B. With 38,387 career points, Kareem retired in 1989 with the NBA career scoring record.

ON CAMPUS

1. WHICH OF THESE COLLEGE FOOTBALL
GREATS DID *NOT* WIN THE HEISMAN TROPHY?

A. Bo Jackson

B. Herschel Walker

C. Joe Theismann

D. Billy Sims

2. WHICH SCHOOL HAS WON THE MOST
NATIONAL CHAMPIONSHIPS IN FOOTBALL?

A. Alabama

B. Notre Dame

C. Oklahoma

D. Princeton

FOOTBALL

1.

C. Though he changed the pronunciation of his name to rhyme with the fabled award while quarterbacking Notre Dame, Theismann was runner-up to Jim Plunkett in the 1970 Heisman voting.

2.

D. You might be surprised to hear it, but Princeton claims 28 national titles—beginning in 1869—although debate exists about the "mythical" nature of those championships.

3. NAME THE LEGENDARY COACH WHO WON
MORE THAN **88** PERCENT OF HIS GAMES.

4. WHO WAS THE FIRST PLAYER TO WIN THE
HEISMAN TROPHY TWICE?

A. Bo Jackson

B. Archie Griffin

C. Charles White

D. Tim Brown

5. TRUE OR FALSE?

Knute Rockne is considered the "father of American
football."

6. WHO WAS THE FIRST FRESHMAN TO WIN THE
HEISMAN TROPHY?

A. Johnny Manziel

B. Charles Woodson

C. Vinny Testaverde

D. Glenn Davis

3.

Knute Rockne. The Notre Dame coach, with a 105–12–5 career mark, holds the record for winning percentage in both the college and pro ranks.

4.

B. Griffin, the Ohio State running back, won the award in 1974 and '75.

5.

False. Walter Camp, who coached at Stanford and Yale, holds that distinction for his role in shaping the game as we know it.

6.

A. In 2013, Texas A&M quarterback "Johnny Football" became the first frosh to win the award.

96

7. WHAT NICKNAME DO THE STADIUMS OF CLEMSON AND LSU SHARE?

---

8. WHICH OF THE FOLLOWING COLLEGE FOOTBALL AWARDS IS GIVEN ANNUALLY TO A DEFENSIVE PLAYER?

A. Maxwell Award

B. Davey O'Brien Award

C. Chuck Bednarik Award

D. Lou Groza Award

9. IN THE ERA OF THE AP POLL (SINCE 1936), WHO WAS THE FIRST COACH TO WIN DIVISION I NATIONAL CHAMPIONSHIPS AT TWO DIFFERENT SCHOOLS?

A. Urban Meyer

B. Jim Tressel

C. Lou Holtz

D. Nick Saban

7.

Death Valley. And debate has gone on for years among fans about which home field is the "true" Death Valley.

8.

C. The Chuck Bednarik Award is given to the Defensive Player of the Year.

9.

D. Saban won titles at LSU and Alabama to earn this distinction.

10. WHAT DOES BCS STAND FOR?

11. WHICH COLLEGE FOOTBALL RIVALRY HAS BEEN PLAYED THE MOST TIMES?

A. Army-Navy

B. Lafayette-Lehigh

C. Notre Dame-Southern Cal

D. Ohio State-Michigan

12. TRUE OR FALSE?

The winner of the annual Army-Navy game is awarded the Commander-in-Chief's Trophy.

13. WHAT ANNUAL GAME IS KNOWN AS THE IRON BOWL?

A. Yale-Princeton

B. Michigan-Notre Dame

C. Auburn-Alabama

D. Army-Navy

10.

Bowl Championship Series

11.

B. These Eastern Pennsylvania neighbors have been doing gridiron battle since 1884.

12.

False. In addition to Army and Navy, Air Force is also eligible in this round-robin competition among service academies.

13.

C. The Auburn-Alabama series dates to 1892, and was named the Iron Bowl in honor of Birmingham, which sits on vast deposits of iron ore.

14. WHICH OF THE FOLLOWING COLLEGE FOOTBALL STARS WENT ON TO PLAY PROFESSIONAL BASKETBALL?

A. Charlie Ward

B. Deion Sanders

C. Joe Montana

D. Bo Jackson

15. WHICH SCHOOL, BY A MARGIN OF ALMOST 100 GAMES, HOLDS THE NCAA RECORD FOR MOST CONSECUTIVE SOLD-OUT HOME GAMES?

16. WHICH COLLEGE FOOTBALL RIVALRY, THANKS TO ITS TAILGATE PARTIES, IS AFFECTIONATELY KNOWN AS THE "WORLD'S LARGEST OUTDOOR COCKTAIL PARTY"?

A. LSU-Alabama

B. Ohio State-Michigan

C. Texas-Texas A&M

D. Florida-Georgia

14.

A. While Sanders and Jackson played pro baseball, it was Florida State's Ward who starred on the hardwood for the New York Knicks.

15.

Nebraska. The Cornhuskers sold out against Missouri in 1962 and have not had an unsold seat since.

16.

D. The SEC rivalry between the Gators and Bulldogs inspires this refreshing moniker.

17. ONLY 11 PLAYERS ARE ALLOWED ON THE FIELD AT A TIME, BUT WHICH SCHOOL GOES ALL-OUT TO CELEBRATE ITS "12TH MAN" TRADITION?

A. Texas

B. Texas A&M

C. Notre Dame

D. Oregon

18. WHICH DIVISION I PROGRAM HAS WON MORE FOOTBALL GAMES THAN ANY OTHER?

19. IN 1982, CAL BEAT STANFORD ON "THE PLAY," THE MOST AMAZING FINISH TO ANY COLLEGE FOOTBALL GAME IN HISTORY. WHO WAS STANFORD'S QUARTERBACK?

A. Jim Plunkett

B. Turk Schonert

C. John Elway

D. Steve Stenstrom

17.

B. Texas A&M allows a distinguished "unsung" player to wear jersey no. 12 in honor of the tradition.

18.

Michigan. In fact, the Wolverines actually taught Notre Dame how to play football in 1887.

19.

C. Elway had driven Stanford to a 20–19 lead in the final minute before Cal returned the ensuing kickoff for the winning touchdown, thanks to the most exciting series of laterals in football history.

20. **TRUE OR FALSE?**

Toledo won the first overtime game in major college football history.

21. **WHICH U.S. STATE WAS HOME TO EVERY NCAA DIVISION I FOOTBALL CHAMPION BETWEEN 2009 AND '12?**

A. Ohio

B. California

C. Louisiana

D. Alabama

22. **AT WHICH UNIVERSITY IS "DOTTING THE 'I'" CONSIDERED TO BE AMONG THE HIGHEST HONORS?**

A. Iowa

B. Ohio State

C. Indiana

D. Wisconsin

20.

True. The Rockets defeated Nevada, 40–37, in the 1995 Las Vegas Bowl in the first OT game since the NCAA adopted the rule.

21.

D. With Alabama winning in 2009, '11 and '12, and Auburn prevailing in '10, the BCS championship trophy never had to travel far.

22.

B. Dotting the "i" in "Script Ohio" is among the great traditions at Ohio State, and considered among the most memorable traditions among marching bands nationwide.

23. WHAT DISTINCTION DOES MICHIGAN'S CHARLES WOODSON HOLD FOR HAVING WON THE 1997 HEISMAN?

24. WHICH SCHOOL'S PLAYERS RUN ONTO THE FIELD BEHIND "RALPHIE," A REAL BUFFALO, IN ONE OF COLLEGE FOOTBALL'S GREAT TRADITIONS?

A. Buffalo

B. Oklahoma

C. Colorado

D. UCLA

25. KNUTE ROCKNE ONCE DIRECTED HIS NOTRE DAME PLAYERS TO "WIN ONE FOR THE GIPPER." WHO PLAYED THE GIPPER, GEORGE GIPP, IN THE 1940 FILM *KNUTE ROCKNE ALL AMERICAN*?

A. Ronald Reagan

B. James Stewart

C. Humphrey Bogart

D. Pat O'Brien

23.

Woodson was the first mostly-defensive player to ever win the award. The defensive back did return kicks and take snaps at receiver, but his primary position was on defense for the Wolverines.

24.

C. The Colorado Buffaloes have been running behind a live buffalo since 1967.

25.

A. Some 40 years before he became 40th president of the United States, Ronald Reagan played one of Notre Dame's greatest football heroes.

GOING PRO

1. AFTER SUFFERING A SERIOUS KNEE INJURY IN 2011, WHICH RUNNING BACK MADE AN AMAZING COMEBACK TO LEAD THE NFL WITH A NEAR-RECORD 2,097 RUSHING YARDS AND 2,314 YARDS FROM SCRIMMAGE IN 2012?

A. Adrian Peterson

B. Jamaal Charles

C. Marshawn Lynch

D. Doug Martin

2. NAME THE KICKER WHO LED ALL NFL SCORERS IN 1998 WHILE MAKING EVERY SINGLE FIELD GOAL AND EXTRA-POINT ATTEMPT, HELPING HIS TEAM LEAD THE LEAGUE IN TOTAL POINTS.

A. Morten Andersen

B. Gary Anderson

C. Steve Christie

D. Al Del Greco

1.

A. Peterson came within nine yards of Eric Dickerson's single-season rushing record in his stunning return to the Minnesota Vikings.

2.

B. Anderson enjoyed a perfect season for the Minnesota Vikings by going 35-for-35 on field goals and 59-for-59 on extra points, totaling 164 points.

3. **WHICH PLAYER, DURING THE 1980S, '90S AND 2000S, SET VIRTUALLY EVERY SUPER BOWL RECEIVING RECORD?**

4. **DESPITE LEADING THE NFL IN NUMBER OF TIMES BEING SACKED, WHICH PLAYER POSTED THE HIGHEST QB RATING DURING THE 2012 REGULAR SEASON?**

   A. Eli Manning

   B. Russell Wilson

   C. Aaron Rodgers

   D. Peyton Manning

5. **TRUE OR FALSE?**

   Brett Favre owns the record for longest touchdown pass in Super Bowl history, an 81-yard strike to Antonio Freeman.

3.

Jerry Rice of the San Francisco 49ers, and later the Oakland Raiders, set records for catches, yards, and receiving touchdowns in a game and career.

4.

C. Rodgers was sacked a league-leading 51 times in 2012, but still posted a QB rating of 108 while leading his injury-depleted Packers to an NFC North crown.

5.

False. Favre did set the record with that pass to Freeman in 1997, but seven years later Carolina Panthers QB Jake Delhomme broke it with an 85-yard scoring pass to Muhsin Muhammad.

6. **WHEN HE STARTED HIS 117TH CONSECUTIVE GAME IN 1999, WHICH PLAYER DID BRETT FAVRE OVERTAKE TO BECOME THE NEW NFL "IRON MAN"?**

A. Dan Marino

B. Terry Bradshaw

C. Joe Ferguson

D. Ron Jaworski

7. **TRUE OR FALSE?**

The 1972 Miami Dolphins are the only team to have gone undefeated during an NFL regular season.

8. **WHICH RUNNING BACK WAS THE FIRST PLAYER TO RUSH FOR 20 TOUCHDOWNS IN A SINGLE SEASON?**

A. John Riggins

B. Emmitt Smith

C. Chuck Muncie

D. Joe Morris

6.

D. Ron Jaworski set the previous mark of 116 games before breaking his leg in 1984. By the time Favre officially retired in 2011, he had stretched the record to 297 games in a row.

7.

False. The 2007 New England Patriots went 16–0. While the Dolphins went on to win it all, however, the Patriots lost to the New York Giants in the Super Bowl, ensuring another annual champagne toast for Coach Don Shula and his '72 players.

8.

A. Riggins, still bruising at 34 years old, ran for 24 touchdowns for the Washington Redskins in 1983.

9. WHEN THE PACKERS AND SEAHAWKS MET DURING WEEK 3 OF THE 2012 SEASON, THE "REPLACEMENT" REFEREES FOUND THEMSELVES IN QUITE A PREDICAMENT REGARDING THE GAME-WINNING DRIVE. WHO WAS RULED TO HAVE SCORED THE WINNING TOUCHDOWN ON WHAT SOME DUBBED THE "FAIL MARY"?

A. Aaron Rodgers

B. Marshawn Lynch

C. Golden Tate

D. Cedric Benson

10. WITH "TERRIBLE TOWELS" WAVING ALL AROUND HIM, WHO WAS THE FIRST QUARTERBACK TO WIN FOUR SUPER BOWL CHAMPIONSHIPS?

11. NAME THE FIRST TEAM TO WIN FIVE SUPER BOWL CHAMPIONSHIPS.

9.

C. Tate was ruled to have caught the ball, even though it appeared that Packers safety M.D. Jennings had made an interception of Russell Wilson's desperation pass. This play was a catalyst in the deal that was struck between the NFL and its referees, getting the regulars back under contract.

10.

Terry Bradshaw led the Pittsburgh Steelers to four Super Bowl wins during a six-year stretch beginning with the 1974 NFL season.

11.

The San Francisco 49ers were the "Team of the 1980s" with four Super Bowl titles that decade, and they added a fifth after the 1994 season. The following year, the Dallas Cowboys won their fifth. And the Pittsburgh Steelers passed both of them with fifth and sixth Super Bowl crowns in the 2000s.

12. WHICH OF THE FOLLOWING QUARTERBACKS DID *NOT* PLAY IN A SUPER BOWL FOR THE SAN FRANCISCO 49ERS?

A. Steve Young

B. Joe Montana

C. Rich Gannon

D. Colin Kaepernick

13. TRUE OR FALSE?

The Chicago Bears have won more NFL games than any team in history.

14. OVER HIS FIRST 10 NFL SEASONS, ATLANTA FALCONS COACH MIKE SMITH WON 70 PERCENT OF HIS GAMES. WHICH OF THE FOLLOWING FORMER COACHES WAS *NOT* ONE OF THE FOUR AHEAD OF HIM ON THE CAREER WINNING PERCENTAGE LIST?

A. John Madden

B. Vince Lombardi

C. George Allen

D. Don Shula

12.

C. Gannon played in a Super Bowl for another Bay Area team, the Oakland Raiders, while the other three were Super Bowl QBs for the San Francisco 49ers.

13.

True. The Chicago Bears have been racking up wins since 1920, and after the 2012 season had 32 more wins than their nearest rival, the Green Bay Packers.

14.

D. While Shula is in the top 10 with a 67.8-percent success rate, the longtime Miami Dolphins coach is not above the 70-percent mark.

15. WHICH QUARTERBACK CAME BACK FROM WHAT SOME THOUGHT WOULD BE A CAREER-ENDING NECK INJURY TO MAKE THE NFL ALL-PRO TEAM IN 2012?

16. WHICH LEGENDARY FOOTBALL INNOVATOR WAS AFFECTIONATELY KNOWN AS "PAPA BEAR"?

A. Bear Bryant

B. George Halas

C. George Allen

D. Pop Warner

17. TRUE OR FALSE?

Kurt Warner is the only QB to have won the Super Bowl with two different teams.

15.

Peyton Manning defied the odds to become one of the greatest comeback stories of the year, returning from a serious injury with the Indianapolis Colts to lead the Denver Broncos to a 13–3 record.

16.

B. Halas, a league founder, owner and coach of the Chicago Bears for more than 40 years, earned that nickname during his involvement in the NFL over the league's first half century.

17.

False. While Warner led both the St. Louis Rams and Arizona Cardinals to the Super Bowl, he only came out victorious—and was named Super Bowl MVP—with the 1999 Rams.

18. WHICH OF THE FOLLOWING SUPER BOWL-
WINNING QUARTERBACKS WAS CHOSEN
LOWEST IN THE NFL DRAFT?

A. Joe Montana

B. Joe Flacco

C. Brad Johnson

D. Tom Brady

19. AFTER BEING DRAFTED IN THE 10TH
ROUND IN 1964 AND SERVING A TOUR IN
THE U.S. NAVY, WHICH QUARTERBACK
JOINED THE DALLAS COWBOYS AND
ULTIMATELY TURNED THEM INTO SUPER
BOWL CHAMPIONS?

A. Tony Romo

B. Danny White

C. Drew Bledsoe

D. Roger Staubach

20. WHO, IN 2012, BROKE JOHNNY UNITAS'
LONGSTANDING RECORD FOR CONSECUTIVE
GAMES THROWING AT LEAST ONE
TOUCHDOWN PASS?

18.

C. Flacco was a first-rounder, Montana a third-rounder and Brady a sixth-rounder. Brad Johnson, though, was a ninth-round choice out of Florida State in 1992 who went on to quarterback the 2002 Tampa Bay Buccaneers to a Super Bowl victory.

19.

D. Despite winning the Heisman Trophy at the Naval Academy, Staubach slipped in the draft because of his mandatory military stint but turned out to be the greatest quarterback in franchise history.

20.

Drew Brees. The New Orleans Saints QB threw at least one scoring pass in 54 consecutive games before a November loss to the Atlanta Falcons.

21. EMMITT SMITH BECAME THE NFL'S CAREER RUSHING LEADER DURING HIS BRILLIANT CAREER BETWEEN 1990 AND 2004. WHO PREVIOUSLY HELD THE RECORD?

A. Jim Brown

B. Barry Sanders

C. Walter Payton

D. Tony Dorsett

22. TRUE OR FALSE?

The Buffalo Bills were the first team to lose four Super Bowl games.

23. WHICH OF THE FOLLOWING NFL FRANCHISES ORIGINATED IN THE CITY IN WHICH IT STILL PLAYS?

A. Dallas Cowboys

B. Arizona Cardinals

C. Indianapolis Colts

D. St. Louis Rams

21.

C. Payton was the only man in NFL history to rush for more than 16,000 career yards before Smith came along and topped 18,000.

22.

False. Before the New England Patriots, Buffalo Bills, or Denver Broncos lost their fourth ones, the Minnesota Vikings "accomplished" the dubious feat by losing four of the first 11 Super Bowls played.

23.

A. The Cowboys were founded in Dallas in 1960. The Cardinals were born in Chicago and moved to St. Louis; the Colts started in Baltimore; and the Rams wound up in St. Louis via Cleveland and Los Angeles.

124

24. FANS OF WHICH **NFL** TEAM MIGHT BE FOUND IN THE "DAWG POUND" AT HOME GAMES?

A. Cincinnati Bengals

B. Pittsburgh Steelers

C. Cleveland Browns

D. Houston Texans

25. THOUGH HE PLAYED ONLY NINE SEASONS, WHICH HALL OF FAME RUNNING BACK WAS NAMED **NFL MVP** THREE TIMES AND AVERAGED AN AMAZING **5.2** YARDS PER CARRY DURING HIS CAREER?

24.

C. Rabid fans in the bleacher seats at Cleveland Browns games refer to their area as the "Dawg Pound."

25.

Jim Brown. The Cleveland Browns great led the NFL in rushing in all but one of his nine campaigns.

REGULAR SEASON

1. WHICH OF THE FOLLOWING TEAMS WAS NOT ONE OF THE NHL'S "ORIGINAL SIX" FRANCHISES?

A. Boston Bruins

B. Chicago Blackhawks

C. Montreal Canadiens

D. Philadelphia Flyers

2. ON NOVEMBER 1, 1959, WHICH GOALTENDER WAS THE FIRST IN NHL HISTORY TO WEAR A FULL PROTECTIVE MASK?

A. Ken Dryden

B. Jacques Plante

C. Clint Benedict

D. Glenn Hall

1.

D. The Philadelphia Flyers arrived in the NHL's 1967 expansion. In addition to Chicago, Montreal, and Boston, the Original Six included the New York Rangers, Toronto Maple Leafs, and Detroit Red Wings.

2.

B. After taking a puck to the face that split his lip, Plante went to the locker room for stitches and returned with the facemask. It initially prompted ridicule, but soon caught on among other goalies and became the norm. Benedict had worn a half-mask for a brief time in 1930 to protect injuries, but said it blocked his vision and scrapped it after a few games.

3. WHAT THREE "STATISTICS" COMPRISE A "GORDIE HOWE HAT TRICK"?

4. TRUE OR FALSE?

Wayne Gretzky is the all-time NHL leader in goals, assists, and points.

5. WHICH COACH TOPS THE NHL CAREER VICTORY LIST?

A. Scotty Bowman

B. Mike Keenan

C. Al Arbour

D. Dick Irvin

6. NAME THE NHL GOALIE WHO IS MORE THAN 100 AHEAD OF HIS NEAREST RIVAL ATOP THE CAREER WIN LIST.

3.

A goal, an assist, and a fight in the same game comprise a "Gordie Howe hat trick," a nod to the kind of effort that was not unfamiliar to the longtime Detroit Red Wings great.

4.

True, and it's not even close. "The Great One" totaled 894 goals and 1,963 assists for 2,857 points—almost 1,000 more than his closest rival.

5.

A. Bowman, with 1,244 career victories, is the only coach in NHL history with more than 1,000.

6.

Martin Brodeur. The fixture between the pipes for the New Jersey Devils is the only goalie with more than 600 career victories.

7. **WHICH TEAM BEGAN 2012-13 WITH AN NHL RECORD STREAK OF 24 STRAIGHT GAMES WITHOUT A REGULATION-TIME LOSS?**

A. Detroit Red Wings

B. Colorado Avalanche

C. Chicago Blackhawks

D. New York Rangers

8. **WHAT FAMOUS "GOON" HOLDS THE NHL CAREER RECORD WITH 3,966 PENALTY MINUTES?**

A. Tie Domi

B. Tiger Williams

C. Marty McSorley

D. Dale Hunter

9. **TRUE OR FALSE?**

Martin Brodeur is the all-time NHL leader in shutouts.

131

7.

C. The Chicago Blackhawks scored at least one point in 24 straight games to open the season, a feat unmatched in NHL history.

8.

B. While the others were all renowned scrappers in their own right, no one served more penalty time than Dave "Tiger" Williams, who prowled the ice from 1974 to '88.

9.

True. The New Jersey Devils goalie broke Terry Sawchuk's 40-year record with his 104th career shutout in 2009 and has padded the margin substantially since then.

10. WHEN DID THE **NHL** INSTITUTE THE SHOOTOUT TO DETERMINE THE OUTCOME OF GAMES TIED AFTER OVERTIME?

A. 1995

B. 2000

C. 2005

D. 2010

11. WHAT TROPHY IS GIVEN ANNUALLY TO THE **NHL** PLAYER WHO BEST DEMONSTRATES "SPORTSMANSHIP AND GENTLEMANLY CONDUCT," ALONG WITH A HIGH STANDARD OF PLAY?

12. WHO WAS THE HIGHEST-SCORING DEFENSEMAN IN **NHL** HISTORY?

A. Bobby Orr

B. Ray Bourque

C. Denis Potvin

D. Al MacInnis

10.

C. It was upon returning from a labor dispute in November 2005 that the NHL introduced the shootout to decide games still tied after a 5-minute overtime period.

11.

The Lady Byng Memorial Trophy. Pavel Datsyuk of the Detroit Red Wings won it three years in row from 2006 to '09.

12.

B. Ray Bourque set NHL records for defensemen with 410 goals, 1,169 assists, and 1,579 points between 1979 and 2001.

13. **WHAT IS UNIQUE ABOUT THE NHL WINTER CLASSIC SERIES?**

14. **WHICH OF THE FOLLOWING TEAMS DID *NOT* JOIN THE NHL IN THE 1990S?**

A. Winnipeg Jets

B. Tampa Bay Lightning

C. Ottawa Senators

D. San Jose Sharks

15. **TRUE OR FALSE?**

The Art Ross Trophy is given annually to the best player in NCAA Division I college hockey.

16. **WHAT'S THE LONGEST-RUNNING RIVALRY IN NHL HISTORY?**

A. Toronto-Detroit

B. Philadelphia-Pittsburgh

C. Boston-Montreal

D. St. Louis-Chicago

13.

It is played outdoors. Inspired by a college game between Michigan and Michigan State that drew 104,173 fans to Michigan Stadium in 2010, the NHL began scheduling annual outdoor games.

14.

A. The Winnipeg Jets joined the NHL from the WHA in the 1970s and played until '96, then came back to life in 2012-13 when the Atlanta Thrashers moved north.

15.

False. The Art Ross Trophy goes to the player who leads the NHL in points. The top college player receives the Hobey Baker Award.

16.

C. The Boston Bruins and Montreal Canadiens, in addition to their many postseason meetings, have been doing battle since 1924.

17. WHICH HARD-SHOOTING CHICAGO
BLACKHAWKS LEGEND, NICKNAMED THE
"GOLDEN JET," ALSO GAVE THE NHL THE
"GOLDEN BRETT" IN THE FORM OF HIS
SUPERSTAR SON?

18. WHICH OF THE FOLLOWING GREATS IS *NOT*
A MEMBER OF THE MONTREAL CANADIENS'
RING OF HONOR?

A. Ken Dryden

B. Larry Robinson

C. Maurice Richard

D. Stan Mikita

19. FOR SEVEN STRAIGHT SEASONS BETWEEN
1969 AND '75, A BOSTON BRUIN LED THE
NHL IN SCORING. FIVE OF THOSE TIMES,
IT WAS PHIL ESPOSITO. WHICH HALL OF
FAME DEFENSEMAN ACCOUNTED FOR THE
OTHER TWO?

17.

Bobby Hull. Hull scored 610 NHL goals. His son, Brett, tallied 741.

18.

D. While the others powered the Montreal Canadiens to dynasty status, Mikita was a Chicago Blackhawks legend.

19.

Bobby Orr. Despite his role as a "blue liner," the sensational Orr led the NHL in total points in 1969-70 and '74-75.

20. Who, in 1975-76, became the first Montreal Canadiens player to win the NHL scoring title since Bernie "Boom Boom" Geoffrion 15 years earlier?

A. Steve Shutt

B. Guy LaFleur

C. Yvan Cournoyer

D. Bob Gainey

21. True or false?

The Canada Cup hockey series began as a tournament pitting the best players from Canada against the best from the United States.

22. Which Hall of Famer, two years after retiring, returned to the ice in his mid-40s to suit up for the WHA's Houston Aeros with his sons, Mark and Marty, and wound up winning the WHA scoring title?

139

20.

B. LaFleur began a string of three consecutive years as the NHL's top point-getter.

21.

False. The tournament got its origin in 1972 as a series between the best from Canada and the top players from the Soviet Union. It was later renamed the World Cup of Hockey and expanded to include other countries.

22.

Gordie Howe. Howe wound up playing six WHA seasons, and later returned to the NHL at age 51 as Mark's teammate with the Hartford Whalers in 1979-80.

23. WHICH OFFENSIVE-MINDED TWINS GAVE VANCOUVER FANS TWICE AS MUCH TO CHEER ABOUT BY WINNING BACK-TO-BACK NHL SCORING TITLES IN 2009-10 AND '10-11?

24. WHO, DURING 2006-07, BECAME THE YOUNGEST PLAYER IN NHL HISTORY TO WIN A SCORING TITLE WHEN HE DID SO AT AGE 20?

A. Sidney Crosby

B. Martin St. Louis

C. Alexander Ovechkin

D. Joe Thornton

25. NAME THE PITTSBURGH PENGUINS GREAT WHO BATTLED HODGKIN'S LYMPHOMA, RETIRED IN 1997, AND MADE AN AMAZING COMEBACK AT AGE 35 IN 2000.

23.

The Sedin twins. Henrik was the NHL's top point-getter in '09-10 and twin brother Daniel accomplished the same feat the following season.

24.

A. "Sid the Kid" also became the youngest player in NHL history to reach 200 career points that season.

25.

Mario Lemieux. Lemieux retired for good in 2006, has helped raise millions of dollars for the fight against blood cancers, and has been credited with saving NHL hockey in Pittsburgh.

STANLEY CUP PLAYOFFS

1. WHICH NHL FRANCHISE HAS WON THE MOST STANLEY CUPS?

A. Boston Bruins

B. Detroit Red Wings

C. Toronto Maple Leafs

D. Montreal Canadiens

2. HOW MUCH DID LORD STANLEY OF PRESTON, THEN THE GOVERNOR GENERAL OF CANADA, PAY FOR THE STANLEY CUP IN 1893?

A. $50

B. $100

C. $200

D. $500

3. NAME THE FORMER EDMONTON OILERS STANLEY CUP CHAMPION WHO, IN 1993-94, TREATED NEW YORK RANGERS FANS TO THEIR FIRST STANLEY CUP CHAMPIONSHIP CELEBRATION SINCE 1940?

1.

D. With 24 Stanley Cup titles between 1915-16 and 1992-93, the Montreal Canadiens have a comfortable margin over their nearest competitors, the Toronto Maple Leafs.

2.

A. For a mere $50, the trophy that would become one of the most storied in sports was bought as a prize to be awarded to the top amateur hockey club in Canada.

3.

Mark Messier. He totaled 12 goals and 18 assists in the postseason in leading the Rangers to the title—his sixth Stanley Cup as a player.

4. THE CONN SMYTHE TROPHY IS GIVEN TO THE MVP OF THE STANLEY CUP PLAYOFFS. WHO, IN 1991 AND '92, BECAME THE FIRST PLAYER TO WIN IT IN BACK-TO-BACK YEARS SINCE BERNIE PARENT OF THE PHILADELPHIA FLYERS IN THE 1970S?

A. Wayne Gretzky

B. Mario Lemieux

C. Steve Yzerman

D. Patrick Roy

5. WHICH TEAM OPENED THE 1980S BY WINNING FOUR CONSECUTIVE STANLEY CUP TITLES?

A. Edmonton Oilers

B. Montreal Canadiens

C. New York Islanders

D. Boston Bruins

6. KEN DRYDEN PLAYED GOALIE FOR THE MONTREAL CANADIENS FOR EIGHT SEASONS. HOW MANY STANLEY CUPS DID HE WIN?

145

4.

B. Lemieux earned the award after leading the Pittsburgh Penguins to each of their consecutive Cups.

5.

C. Al Arbour's New York Islanders. While the Edmonton Oilers won four Cups in a five-year stretch of the 1980s and five over seven years, it was the "Isles" who strung together four straight.

6.

Six. Dryden won his first as a rookie in 1970-71 after playing just six games in the regular season. He added five more titles, including one in each of his last four seasons.

7. **WHO WAS THE FIRST COACH TO WIN STANLEY CUP TITLES WITH THREE DIFFERENT TEAMS?**

A. Glen Sather

B. Hector "Toe" Blake

C. Jacques Demers

D. Scotty Bowman

8. **TRUE OR FALSE?**

The top three career scorers in Stanley Cup playoff history skated for the Edmonton Oilers.

9. **WHICH GOALIE WON THE CONN SMYTHE TROPHY THREE TIMES, AND WITH TWO DIFFERENT TEAMS?**

A. Billy Smith

B. Patrick Roy

C. Martin Brodeur

D. Glenn Hall

7.

D. Bowman took the Montreal Canadiens to five Stanley Cups and the Pittsburgh Penguins and Detroit Red Wings to two apiece.

8.

True. Wayne Gretzky, Mark Messier, and Jari Kurri—all members of an Edmonton Oilers dynasty that won five Stanley Cups in seven years—are the top three point-getters in playoff history.

9.

B. Roy won the award as postseason MVP with the Montreal Canadiens in 1986 and '93 and again with the Colorado Avalanche in 2001.

10. **Who was the first American-born player to win the Conn Smythe Trophy as MVP of the Stanley Cup playoffs?**

A. Brian Leetch

B. Jonathan Quick

C. Tim Thomas

D. Mike Modano

11. **Which team set a Stanley Cup playoff record by winning 10 consecutive road games on the way to claiming the 2012 Stanley Cup?**

A. San Jose Sharks

B. Los Angeles Kings

C. Vancouver Canucks

D. Philadelphia Flyers

12. **True or false?**

No women have their name inscribed on the Stanley Cup.

10.

A. Leetch, of the New York Rangers, became the first American winner of the Conn Smythe Trophy in 1994. Thomas and Quick became the second and third, respectively, in 2011 and '12.

11.

B. The Los Angeles Kings won their first 10 road games of the 2012 Stanley Cup playoffs and clinched their first Cup with a 16–4 overall run through the postseason.

12.

False. Several do, mainly as team owners and executives. The first woman to have her name on the Cup was Detroit Red Wings president Marguerite Norris in 1955.

13. WHICH DEFENSEMAN FAMOUSLY FLEW THROUGH THE AIR AFTER SCORING THE CLINCHING GOAL IN OVERTIME TO LIFT THE BOSTON BRUINS TO A STANLEY CUP VICTORY OVER THE ST. LOUIS BLUES IN 1970?

14. NAME THE PLAYER WHO SET AN NHL RECORD BY MAKING THE STANLEY CUP PLAYOFFS IN 24 DIFFERENT SEASONS.

A. Ray Bourque

B. Larry Robinson

C. Steve Yzerman

D. Chris Chelios

15. WHOSE NAME APPEARS THE MOST TIMES ON THE STANLEY CUP?

A. Guy LaFleur

B. Wayne Gretzky

C. Mark Messier

D. Jean Beliveau

13.

Bobby Orr. A statue commemorating the moment was unveiled in Boston in 2010 on the 40th anniversary of Orr's unforgettable flight.

14.

D. While all of the players listed made the playoffs at least 20 times, Chelios set the NHL record with 24 appearances. He represented the Chicago Blackhawks, Detroit Red Wings, and Montreal Canadiens.

15.

D. Beliveau, the former Montreal Canadiens great, has his name on the Cup 17 times—10 as a player and seven as an executive.

SUMMER GAMES

1. HOW LONG WAS THE FIRST OLYMPIC MARATHON IN 1896?

    A. 20 miles

    B. 24.8 miles

    C. 26.2 miles

    D. 30 miles

2. TEAM USA HAS DOMINATED MEN'S BASKETBALL PLAY IN THE OLYMPIC GAMES, BUT WHICH COUNTRY WON THE GOLD MEDAL IN 2004?

3. NAME THE AMERICAN TRACK AND FIELD SUPERSTAR WHO WON FOUR CONSECUTIVE OLYMPIC LONG JUMP GOLD MEDALS FROM 1984 TO '96.

1.

B. While official marathons would later become 26.2 miles, the first one—run from Marathon (hence the name) to Athens as a re-tracing of the steps of the famous Greek messenger Pheidippides—was 24.8 miles. Greece's Spiridon Louis won in just under three hours.

2.

Argentina

3.

Carl Lewis. Lewis matched his hero, Jesse Owens, with four gold medals in the 1984 Games. One of those was in the long jump, which he went on to win at the next three Olympics as well.

4. NAME THE SPRINTER WHO, WITH SIX MEDALS IN THE **1980**S AND '**90**S, BECAME THE MOST DECORATED WOMAN IN U.S. TRACK AND FIELD HISTORY.

A. Gail Devers

B. Marion Jones

C. Florence Griffith-Joyner

D. Jackie Joyner-Kersee

5. IN WHAT YEAR DID BEACH VOLLEYBALL BECOME AN OFFICIAL OLYMPIC SPORT?

A. 1992

B. 1996

C. 2000

D. 2004

6. TRUE OR FALSE?

Los Angeles has hosted the Summer Games twice.

4.

D. Joyner-Kersee has been referred to as the "First Lady of American track and field."

5.

B. Beach volleyball first appeared at the 1996 Summer Olympics in Atlanta. It is now one of the most popular spectator sports at the Summer Olympic Games.

6.

True. L.A. hosted the Games in 1932 and 1984.

7. DURING THE 2012 GAMES, AMERICAN SWIMMER MICHAEL PHELPS RAISED HIS TOTAL TO 22 MEDALS (18 GOLD) TO BECOME THE MOST DECORATED OLYMPIAN OF ALL TIME. WHO HELD THE PREVIOUS MARK FOR MOST MEDALS, REGARDLESS OF SPORT?

A. Mark Spitz

B. Carl Lewis

C. Larisa Latynina

D. Nadia Comaneci

8. NAME THE LEGENDARY GYMNASTICS COACH WHOSE OLYMPIC CHAMPIONS HAVE INCLUDED ROMANIA'S NADIA COMANECI AND AMERICANS MARY LOU RETTON, KERRI STRUG, AND DOMINIQUE MOCEANU.

A. Bela Karolyi

B. Beverly Plocki

C. Amanda Reddin

D. Cathy Rigby

7.

C. Latynina, a Soviet-era gymnast, accumulated 18 Olympic medals.

8.

A. Karolyi, who began his career in Romania before taking over Team USA in 1984, is the most successful gymnastics coach in Olympic history.

9. **AFTER SUFFERING HIS FIRST LOSS AS A COLLEGIAN DURING THE CHAMPIONSHIP MATCH OF HIS FINAL NCAA TOURNAMENT, WHICH WRESTLING LEGEND CRUISED TO A GOLD MEDAL IN THE 1972 OLYMPICS WITHOUT SURRENDERING A SINGLE POINT IN ANY MATCH?**

A. Rulon Gardner

B. Bruce Baumgartner

C. Tom Brands

D. Dan Gable

10. **WHY WERE THE 1972 MUNICH OLYMPIC GAMES SUSPENDED FOR ABOUT 34 HOURS?**

11. **AFTER MORE THAN 60 YEARS, TENNIS WAS REINSTATED AS AN OLYMPIC MEDAL SPORT FOR THE 1988 GAMES IN SEOUL. WHO WON THE WOMEN'S SINGLES TITLE THAT YEAR?**

A. Jennifer Capriati

B. Steffi Graf

C. Martina Navratilova

D. Pam Shriver

9.

D. Gable, who enjoyed unprecedented success as both an athlete and college coach, made one of the most amazing runs in Olympic history by shutting out each of his 1972 Olympic opponents.

10.

Because of a hostage crisis. Palestinian terrorists broke into the Israeli quarters, killed two Israeli athletes, and took nine hostages. Those hostages were later killed in a failed rescue attempt.

11.

B. Graf, then representing West Germany, defeated Gabriela Sabatini in the final.

12. WHAT'S THE LAST NAME OF THE AMERICAN BROTHER DUO FROM ST. LOUIS THAT BROUGHT HOME TWO OLYMPIC BOXING GOLD MEDALS FROM THE MONTREAL GAMES IN 1976?

13. NAME THE AMERICAN DIVER WHO BECAME THE FIRST MAN IN OLYMPIC HISTORY TO SWEEP BOTH THE 3-METER SPRINGBOARD AND 10-METER PLATFORM GOLD MEDALS IN BACK-TO-BACK GAMES.

A. Bob Webster

B. Gary Tobian

C. Greg Louganis

D. David Boudia

14. WHICH EVENT IS *NOT* ONE OF THE SEVEN THAT COMPRISE THE WOMEN'S OLYMPIC HEPTATHLON?

A. Mile run

B. 100 hurdles

C. Shot put

D. Javelin

161

12.

Spinks. Leon won the light heavyweight division gold medal while Michael ruled the middleweight class. Sugar Ray Leonard also won gold for the U.S. that year. Other famous U.S. boxing gold medalists have included George Foreman (1968), Joe Frazier (1964), and Muhammad Ali (1960, as Cassius Clay).

13.

C. Louganis, considered the greatest American diver of all time, won gold in both events in 1984 and '88.

14.

A. The longest running event in the heptathlon covers 800 meters. The seven events are the 100 hurdles, 200 meters, 800 meters, shot put, javelin, high jump, and long jump.

15. WHICH OF THE FOLLOWING U.S. SWIMMING GREATS WON THE FEWEST OLYMPIC MEDALS?

A. Dara Torres

B. Natalie Coughlin

C. Jenny Thompson

D. Mark Spitz

16. DURING THE TIME BASEBALL WAS PLAYED AS AN OLYMPIC MEDAL SPORT BETWEEN 1992 AND 2008, WHICH COUNTRY WON THE MOST GOLD?

A. USA

B. Cuba

C. Japan

D. South Korea

17. WHICH SPORT, WHICH WAS PLAYED IN THE 1900 AND 1904 OLYMPICS, WAS REINSTATED AFTER MORE THAN A CENTURY HIATUS FOR THE 2016 SUMMER GAMES IN RIO?

15.

D. Though he set a record (since broken by Michael Phelps) with seven gold medals in a single Olympics, Spitz falls below the women listed in career medals with 11. Through the 2012 London Games, Torres, Coughlin, and Thompson had each won 12.

16.

B. Cuba won three of the five gold medals during that span. Team USA (2000) and South Korea (2008) won one each.

17.

Golf. When it was last contested in the Olympics in 1904, only two countries—the United States and Canada—took part.

WINTER GAMES

1. WHEN AND WHERE WERE THE FIRST WINTER OLYMPIC GAMES PLAYED?

A. 1920 in Innsbruck, Austria

B. 1924 in Chamonix, France

C. 1928 in St. Moritz, Switzerland

D. 1932 in Lake Placid, New York

2. TRUE OR FALSE?

The first Winter Games were, at the time, referred to not as the Olympics but rather as "International Winter Sports Week."

3. IN WHAT YEAR DID THE UNITED STATES WIN ITS FIRST GOLD MEDAL IN OLYMPIC ICE HOCKEY?

A. 1960

B. 1968

C. 1972

D. 1980

1.

B. The first Winter Games drew athletes to the French Alps in 1924.

2.

True. There were 16 nations on hand, competing in just six different sports.

3.

A. Twenty years before the "Miracle on Ice," Team USA won all seven games to win its first gold on home ice in Squaw Valley, CA in 1960.

4. **WHO SCORED THE WINNING GOAL AGAINST THE SOVIET UNION MIDWAY THROUGH THE THIRD PERIOD WHEN THE AMERICANS PULLED OFF THEIR STUNNING 1980 UPSET?**

A. Herb Brooks

B. Mark Johnson

C. Mike Eruzione

D. Buzz Schneider

5. **TRUE OR FALSE?**

Bode Miller was the first U.S. male skier to win two medals at the same Olympics.

6. **WHO ENTERED THE UNITED STATES FIGURE SKATING HALL OF FAME AS THE MOST DECORATED FIGURE SKATER IN U.S. HISTORY IN 2011 BUT NEVER MANAGED TO WIN A GOLD MEDAL IN THE OLYMPICS?**

A. Tara Lipinski

B. Sarah Hughes

C. Kristi Yamaguchi

D. Michelle Kwan

4.

C. Eruzione, the team captain, broke a 3–3 tie with 10 minutes to play in the 4–3 American shocker.

5.

False. While Miller won three medals (including gold in the super combined) in 2010, raising his career total to five, Tommy Moe earned two medals 16 years earlier in the 1994 Games. He won gold in the downhill and took silver in the super-G.

6.

D. Lipinski, Hughes, and Yamaguchi all won individual gold medals in the Olympics, while Kwan—for all her American and world success—had to settle for silver in 1998 and bronze in 2002.

7. **WHO WAS THE FIRST AMERICAN TO WIN TWO OLYMPIC INDIVIDUAL GOLD MEDALS IN MEN'S FIGURE SKATING?**

A. Dick Button

B. Scott Hamilton

C. Brian Boitano

D. Evan Lysacek

8. **WHAT TWO SPORTS COMPRISE THE OLYMPIC BIATHLON?**

9. **SHE WON A SILVER MEDAL IN THE DOWNHILL IN THE 1994 OLYMPICS. SHE CAME BACK FOUR YEARS LATER TO WIN GOLD IN THE SUPER-G DESPITE SUFFERING A CONCUSSION IN PRACTICE. NAME THIS AMERICAN SKIER WHOSE UNIQUE NAME AND RECKLESS STYLE ENDEARED HER TO FANS.**

10. **TRUE OR FALSE?**

American speed skating star Bonnie Blair won gold medals in three consecutive Olympic Games.

169

7.

A. Button won back-to-back titles in the 1948 and '52 Games. Hamilton and Boitano each won one gold medal in the 1980s, and Lysacek won his first in 2010.

8.

Cross-country skiing and small-caliber rifle shooting. The sport has its roots in ancient hunting practices in northern Europe.

9.

Picabo Street. Her first name means "Shining Waters" in Sho-Ban.

10.

True. Blair, who was inducted into the U.S. Olympic Hall of Fame in 2004, captured the 500 meters at the 1988 games. She then won both the 500 and 1,000 meters in 1992 and '94, finishing her career with five Olympic gold medals.

11. NAME THE AMERICAN SPEED SKATER WHO, IN 1980, BECAME THE *FIRST* ATHLETE IN ANY OLYMPICS—SUMMER OR WINTER—TO WIN FIVE GOLD MEDALS IN ONE GAMES.

12. WHICH FUN-LOVING 1988 OLYMPIC BOBSLED TEAM INSPIRED THE 1993 FILM *COOL RUNNINGS*?

A. Canada

B. Jamaica

C. Norway

D. France

13. NAME THE POPULAR AMERICAN WHO WON HALF-PIPE SNOWBOARDING GOLD MEDALS IN THE 2006 AND 2010 OLYMPIC GAMES.

A. Scotty Lago

B. Ross Powers

C. Shaun White

D. Jarret Thomas

11.

Eric Heiden. The 21-year-old from Wisconsin set Olympic records in all five events, including a world record in the 10,000 meters.

12.

B. The Jamaican bobsled team gained a cult following after qualifying for the Calgary Games.

13.

C. White, the longtime X Games star, used his dazzling aerial moves to score back-to-back Olympic victories.

OTHER SPORTS

1. **WHOSE STREAK OF 11 CONSECUTIVE PGA TOUR VICTORIES IN 1945 IS CONSIDERED NOT ONLY ONE OF THE MOST UNTOUCHABLE RECORDS IN GOLF, BUT IN ALL OF SPORTS?**

A. Sam Snead

B. Byron Nelson

C. Bobby Jones

D. Tiger Woods

2. **WHO IS THE ONLY GOLFER TO HAVE WON THE GRAND SLAM BY CLAIMING ALL FOUR MAJOR TOURNAMENTS IN THE SAME CALENDAR YEAR?**

A. Tiger Woods

B. Jack Nicklaus

C. Arnold Palmer

D. Bobby Jones

1.

B. Nelson won 18 total tournaments that year, and shot 19 consecutive rounds under 70.

2.

D. Jones won the U.S. Amateur, British Amateur, U.S. Open, and British Open in 1930. The four majors have since become the Masters, British Open, U.S. Open, and PGA Championship. Woods won all four consecutively, but not in the same calendar year.

3. TRUE OR FALSE?

Before dominating the PGA Tour as a professional, Tiger Woods became the first player ever to win three consecutive U.S. Amateur championships.

4. WHEN YOU SCORE TWO SHOTS BELOW PAR ON A GOLF HOLE, YOU'VE MADE AN EAGLE. WHAT'S IT CALLED WHEN YOU SHOOT THREE-UNDER PAR ON A SINGLE HOLE?

5. EARLY IN HIS CAREER, TIGER WOODS SET JACK NICKLAUS' PGA RECORD FOR MAJOR CHAMPIONSHIP VICTORIES AS ONE OF HIS FOREMOST GOALS. HOW MANY MAJORS DID NICKLAUS WIN?

A. 12

B. 15

C. 18

D. 21

6. WHAT IS THE NAME OF THE TROPHY GIVEN TO THE WINNING COUNTRY IN THE LARGEST INTERNATIONAL TEAM TENNIS COMPETITION?

3.

True. Woods won in 1994, '95 and '96. Bobby Jones won the U.S. Amateur a record five times, but never three years in a row.

4.

An albatross. You'd need a 2 on a par 5 or a hole in one on a par 4.

5.

C. Nicklaus won 18 majors, beginning with a U.S. Open title as a 22-year-old and ending with a stunning Masters win at age 46 in 1986.

6.

The Davis Cup. The tournament began as a competition between the United States and Great Britain in 1900 but has grown to include some 130 countries.

7. WHICH MEN'S TENNIS GREAT, IN 2012, BROKE PETE SAMPRAS' CAREER RECORD OF 286 WEEKS RANKED NO. 1 IN THE WORLD?

8. WHICH OF THE FOLLOWING IS *NOT* TRUE ABOUT SISTERS VENUS AND SERENA WILLIAMS?

A. Venus is older than Serena.

B. Serena has won more Grand Slam singles titles.

C. They have paired up for several Grand Slam doubles titles.

D. Their first head-to-head Grand Slam final match came at Wimbledon.

9. TRUE OR FALSE?

Arthur Ashe was the first African-American to win Wimbledon.

10. WHICH OF THE FOLLOWING PLAYERS WON THE MOST GRAND SLAM SINGLES TITLES?

A. Bjorn Borg

B. John McEnroe

C. Jimmy Connors

D. Ivan Lendl

7.

Roger Federer. The Swiss star went on to become the first in history with more than 300 weeks spent atop the ATP world rankings.

8.

D. Venus and Serena first squared off in a Grand Slam final at the 2001 U.S. Open. Venus won in straight sets, but Serena took five of their next six meetings in Grand Slam title matches.

9.

False. While Ashe was the first African-American *man* to win Wimbledon, and was also the first to attain the world's No. 1 ranking, it was Althea Gibson's Wimbledon victory back in 1957 that broke the color barrier at the All England Lawn Tennis and Croquet Club.

10.

A. Borg won 11 Grand Slam titles—the French Open six times and Wimbledon five. Lendl and Connors totaled eight titles apiece, while McEnroe collected seven.

11. WHICH COUNTRY WON ITS ALL-TIME LEADING FIFTH WORLD CUP SOCCER TITLE IN 2002?

A. Italy

B. Spain

C. England

D. Brazil

12. TRUE OR FALSE?

A soccer player receiving a yellow card is kicked out of the match.

13. THE UNITED STATES, IN 1950, SCORED A 1–0 VICTORY OVER WHICH COUNTRY IN WHAT WAS CONSIDERED—AT THE TIME— THE BIGGEST UPSET IN INTERNATIONAL SOCCER HISTORY?

A. Italy

B. Mexico

C. England

D. Brazil

179

11.

D. Brazil won its fifth World Cup in 2002. The Brazilians also prevailed in 1958, '62, '70, and '94.

12.

False. A red card means the player must leave the match immediately. A single yellow card serves as a caution, while a subsequent one carries harsher consequences.

13.

C. Joe Gaetjens' goal shocked England in a 1950 World Cup match in Brazil.

14. Name the American professional soccer team that incomparable Brazilian star Pelé came out of retirement to play for in 1975.

15. Muhammad Ali and Joe Frazier battled in three of the greatest heavyweight bouts of all time. What was the nickname given to their classic third bout, won by Ali when Frazier could not answer the bell for the 15th round?

A. Thrilla in Manila

B. Rumble in the Jungle

C. Slugfest in Somalia

D. The Showdown

16. Which boxer, undefeated at the time, was ranked by *Forbes* magazine as the world's highest-paid athlete in 2012?

17. True or false?

In addition to winning 10 world boxing titles in six different weight divisions, Oscar De La Hoya recorded an album that was nominated for a Grammy Award.

14.

The New York Cosmos

15.

A. Manila was the site of the best fight in the trilogy. After his victory, Ali called the pounding he took "the closest thing to dying that I know of."

16.

Floyd Mayweather. In just two huge pay-per-view fights that year, Mayweather held onto his titles and earned $85 million in the process.

17.

True. De La Hoya's self-titled debut album was nominated for Best Latin Pop Album in 2001.

18. NAME THE BOXER WHO SET A WORLD RECORD BY WINNING TITLES IN EIGHT DIFFERENT WEIGHT CLASSES AND WAS NAMED FIGHTER OF THE DECADE FOR THE 2000S BY THE BOXING WRITERS ASSOCIATION OF AMERICA.

A. Floyd Mayweather

B. Manny Pacquiao

C. Oscar De La Hoya

D. Shane Mosley

19. WHICH OF THE FOLLOWING HORSES DID *NOT* WIN THE TRIPLE CROWN?

A. Secretariat

B. Seattle Slew

C. War Admiral

D. Seabiscuit

20. KENTUCKY DERBY, PREAKNESS, OR BELMONT—WHICH IS THE LONGEST OF THE TRIPLE CROWN HORSE RACES?

18.

B. Pacquiao, the pride of The Philippines, took on champion after champion in conquering more weight classes than any fighter in history.

19.

D. Seabiscuit did not hit his stride until after his 3-year-old season, the only year horses are eligible for the Triple Crown series.

20.

The Belmont Stakes, at 1½ miles, is longer than the Derby (1¼ miles) and Preakness (1³⁄₁₆ miles).

21. WHICH ANNUAL EVENT FEATURES THE BEST OF THE BEST IN THOROUGHBRED RACING?

A. Travers Stakes

B. Kentucky Derby

C. Breeders' Cup

D. Ryder Cup

22. WHO, FOR MUCH OF THE 2000S, HAS HELD THE UNOFFICIAL TITLE OF "WORLD'S FASTEST MAN," HAVING RUN THE 100-METER DASH IN A WORLD-RECORD TIME OF 9.58 SECONDS IN GERMANY IN 2009?

23. WHO WAS THE FIRST MAN TO ACCUMULATE $1 MILLION IN CAREER EARNINGS AS A PROFESSIONAL BOWLER?

A. Earl Anthony

B. Walter Ray Williams Jr.

C. Pete Weber

D. Mark Roth

21.

C. While the Kentucky Derby and the Triple Crown races get their share of publicity, those events are only for 3-year-olds. The Breeders' Cup races showcase the top horses of all ages and genders running at various distances.

22.

Jamaican sprinter Usain Bolt, who has also set several Olympic sprinting records.

23.

A. Anthony, a dominant force in the 1970s and '80s, finished with more than $1.4 million in career earnings and a record 41 titles on the regular PBA Tour.

24. IN CYCLING, WHAT COLOR JERSEY GOES TO THE WINNER OF EACH STAGE OF THE TOUR DE FRANCE?

25. SINCE THE NCAA BEGAN AWARDING DIVISION I LACROSSE CHAMPIONSHIPS IN 1971, WHICH SCHOOL HAS WON THE MOST IN MEN'S COMPETITION?

A. Princeton

B. Johns Hopkins

C. Syracuse

D. Virginia

26. THOUGH VOLLEYBALL IS TRADITIONALLY A SPORT DOMINATED BY WESTERN PROGRAMS, WHICH EASTERN SCHOOL WON FOUR CONSECUTIVE WOMEN'S NCAA DIVISION I NATIONAL CHAMPIONSHIPS BETWEEN 2007 AND '10?

A. Duke

B. Penn State

C. North Carolina

D. Rutgers

24.

Yellow. The yellow jersey is considered the Tour's "holy grail."

25.

C. With 11 national titles through 2012, Syracuse has been the most dominant school in men's lacrosse.

26.

B. Penn State became the first school to win four national titles in a row since the NCAA began honoring a Division I champion in 1981.

27. IN WHAT SPORT ARE DUKE KAHANAMOKU, KELLY SLATER, AND LAYNE BEACHLEY CONSIDERED TO RANK AMONG THE GREATEST ATHLETES OF ALL TIME?

28. WHAT CANADIAN CITY ANNUALLY HOSTS THE WORLD'S RICHEST, AND PERHAPS MOST POPULAR, TOURNAMENT-STYLE RODEO?

    A. Toronto

    B. Montreal

    C. Vancouver

    D. Calgary

29. NAME THE SCHOOL THAT BROKE OKLAHOMA STATE'S RECORD BY WINNING NINE CONSECUTIVE NCAA DIVISION I WRESTLING TEAM CHAMPIONSHIPS FROM 1978 TO '86.

    A. Iowa

    B. Iowa State

    C. Minnesota

    D. Penn State

27.

Surfing

28.

D. The Calgary Stampede offers more than $2 million in prize money for the top rodeo cowboys and cowgirls, and draws fans from all over the world.

29.

A. The Dan Gable-coached Hawkeyes surpassed Oklahoma State, which won seven in a row in the 1930s and '40s.

30. WHAT SPORT'S HALL OF FAME INCLUDES THE LIKES OF KEN SHAMROCK, CHUCK LIDDELL, AND RANDY COUTURE?

31. WHICH SPORTS FIGURE HAS *NOT* BEEN FEATURED ON A WHEATIES CEREAL BOX?

A. "Stone Cold" Steve Austin (professional wrestler)

B. Rulon Gardner (Olympic Greco-Roman wrestler)

C. Joe Paterno (college football coach)

D. Esther Williams (swimmer, actress)

32. WHICH SPORT FEATURES PLAYERS USING A CESTA TO THROW A PELOTA AT SPEEDS OF MORE THAN 120 MILES PER HOUR?

A. Jai alai

B. Racquetball

C. Skeet shooting

D. Squash

30.

Ultimate Fighting (UFC or mixed martial arts). Shamrock was one of the early stars in a sport that has grown exponentially in popularity, and one of the first inductees in the UFC Hall of Fame.

31.

B. Gardner never muscled his way onto the box, but Austin, Paterno, and Williams graced breakfast tables across America in 1999, 2003, and 1959, respectively.

32.

A. Jai alai originated in Spain and is not common in the United States, although it does have a large following in Miami. Because pelotas hit the court walls at such high speeds, each has an average life of only about 20 minutes before its cover splits and it needs to be replaced.